Dearest Ophelia —
It seems like yesterday
that we met at our
"first" class. We were soul
friends immediately & always will
be. I am so blessed that you
share this amazing journey of life
with me. You are a bright light
in my life. I love you,
Deb

# Soul-Hearted
# Partnership

# Soul-Hearted Partnership

*Creating the Ultimate Experience of Love, Passion, and Intimacy*

Debra L. Reble, Ph.D.

HeartPaths

CLEVELAND HEIGHTS, OHIO

Published by
HeartPaths Media
Post Office Box 181236
Cleveland Heights, OH 44118
www.soulheartedpartnership.com

Editor: Ellen Kleiner
Book design: David Skolkin
Cover art: Brian Gillen

Text copyright © 2010 by Debra L Reble

Printed in Canada

**Cataloging-in-Publication Data**
Reble, Debra L.
Soul-hearted partnership : creating the ultimate experience of love,
passion, and intimacy / Debra L. Reble, Ph.D. -- Cleveland Heights,
OH : HeartPaths Media, 2009.
p. ; cm.
ISBN: 978-0-9824040-1-0 (pbk.) 978-0-9824040-2-7 (hbk.)
Summary: The movement toward soul-hearted partnership entails developing a fully realized relationship first with ourselves and then with another person. This dynamic, combined with an awareness of our own spiritual progression, helps individuals create a partnership that permits optimum fulfillment of each party, as well as the relationship itself. This is a book for individuals and couples seeking relationship as a means toward spiritual growth.
1. Love. 2. Interpersonal relationships. 3. Mate selection. 4. Soul mates. 5. Spiritual formation. I. Title.
BF575.L8 R43 2009                    2009924872
646.77--dc22 0909

10  9  8  7  6  5  4  3  2  1

With infinite love and gratitude
to the rose of my heart—
my dear husband and soul-hearted partner

*In gratitude . . .*

SPECIAL COLLEAGUES, FRIENDS, AND FAMILY members have been instrumental in making my dream of this book a reality:

Bryan Christopher, my spiritual mentor, soul-hearted friend, and colleague for over twenty-two years, whose love, light, and ideas were invaluable in creating this book;

Ellen Kleiner, whose editorial vision and support, unending enthusiasm and encouragement, and caring guidance when I wanted to give up allowed me to persevere and do my most creative work;

David Skolkin, book designer and dearest friend, without whose extraordinary creative energy, love, and open heart this book would not exist in its exquisite form;

Brian Gillen, cover artist, for bringing the concept of soul hearted to life;

Christy Carlson, who asked me to write a book on personal transformation in the first place and who assisted in editing its first draft;

Bunny Breslin, who provided a trained literary eye, editorial assistance, and a wonderful sense of humor;

Dick Blake, my professional development coach and dance teacher, whose impeccable guidance and support have been enormously valuable;

The amazing clients I have worked with, whose dedication to spiritual growth, constructive feedback, and life-changing results inspired me to develop this material;

My dear friends, the rare gems in my life, who have stood by me with patience, encouragement, and openness to possibility during the four years I spent writing this book;

My son, Thomas, and my daughter, Alexandra, whose incandescent light and energies have facilitated my own transformation and who have inspired me to be a better person;

My father, a blessing in my life and my greatest cheerleader, whether or not my perspectives have agreed with his own;

My stepmother, Barb, who has supported me wholeheartedly;

And finally, my dear husband, Doug, who believed in me even when I stopped believing in myself and whom I love with all my heart.

# Contents

# Preface

*M*Y VISION OF SOUL-HEARTED PARTNERSHIP, which involves first having a fully realized relationship with oneself and then cocreating a soul-connected relationship with another individual, has evolved over twenty-two years of being a teacher, psychologist, relationship counselor, and spiritual guide. The concept of soul-hearted partnership coalesced in January 2000 when I was faced with a pivotal decision about the direction of my life for the new millennium. As I waited at the airport to board a flight to Washington, D.C., to attend a director's retreat for Foundation in Light, I wondered how my life would be affected by accepting a position as codirector of this nonprofit foundation dedicated to empowering people toward self-realization.

Sitting on a black airport bench, I felt like my feet were on the ground anchoring me in my current life, while the rest of me was spinning out of control into my future. At the time, I was depressed, having long been unhappy with my life but not allowing myself to feel the depth of my pain or envision alternative choices. As I waited, I said to myself, "This is not the life I've imagined."

Since my daughter had been born over nine years before, I had felt as if I had been in emotional and spiritual limbo, going through the motions in my second marriage and my work as a psychologist in a mental health agency, always setting my own needs and dreams aside for those of others. I knew that in the past I had compromised myself by playing the role of caretaker in relationships, keeping everything working to make others happy. But in choosing to make other people's lives wonderful, I had forfeited my own fulfillment and my dream of true partnership with myself and a beloved one.

Fortunately, by this time my experience with Foundation in Light had put me in touch with my true being, making me aware of how I had suspended my own life by losing my connection to the divine source that guided me. I now felt that I was on the brink of a major change, as I heard an inner voice I had stifled for more than a decade whispering about living not just an ordinary life but an extraordinary one, as well as realizing my dreams of soul partnership with myself and a beloved partner. Observing the door in the waiting area that would lead to the aircraft, I imagined it to be a portal to new possibilities and that by passing through it I could let go of my past and move into my future of living a fulfilling life by no longer compromising myself or my dreams.

When the flight attendant's voice began calling rows for boarding, my world seemed to stop, catching me in suspended animation as I reviewed how I had come to this turning point. Instantly, I was transported back to the living room of my family's black-and-white center hall colonial on the night of my second husband's doctoral graduation party. I saw him wearing a king's crown made of paper, beaming triumphantly as friends and family congratulated him on his accomplishment while I watched the events, not even as queen, taking a backseat, as always.

Now I understood clearly how I had deferred my life for my partner's in another self-sacrificial relationship in which I played the role of caretaker. I had supported all of my husband's dreams without requesting support for manifesting my own, since I was too busy trying to fix the relationship, which made me feel worthwhile and in control. I also saw that I could not have expected support from others when I had given up supporting myself. I had created a familiar scenario—anticipating that a relationship would complete me—and ironically now we led parallel but separate lives linked only through children and the house. In this graveyard of a marriage, all that initiated our relationship had long been snuffed out and there grew a destructive kudzu vine of indifference that suppressed even discontent. It became crystal clear to me that neither of us had developed a fully realized relationship with ourselves, and thus we could not have a fully realized relationship with each other. This was, I now discovered, largely because I had not followed my soul's path and kept my eye on my own dreams but instead lived in passive coexistence.

From the perspective of my friends and family, my life appeared ideal. They saw the trappings of a comfortable home, two healthy, well-adjusted children, and a marriage free of external conflict. But what they observed was a facade. I had tried to pretend that I could make my marriage work by taking care of everything, a deception my friends and family had encouraged. They supported me as long as I persevered trying to keep the relationship alive even when it had died emotionally and spiritually. And instead of listening to my inner self, I had deferred to everyone else and their ideas of what was best for me. Afraid of disappointing my family and friends, I had avoided the choice I knew my heart had already made.

Yet even though I was living in the shadow of my marriage's death, I knew I had not died with it, because compromising my true being was not an option anymore. In contrast to my past tendency to expect a Prince Charming to ride up on a white horse and make me feel whole before I could live in true partnership with someone, I was aware that I had to have a fulfilling partnership with myself. I had to first create what was missing in my own life and love myself without reservation before I could share with another person a fully realized partnership.

As I boarded the plane, I knew that by committing myself to attending the retreat I was choosing to follow my dreams and fulfill my soul's journey. I affirmed my ability to love, trust, and fully express my being, then to have a loving and fulfilling relationship with a partner. By the time the plane had taken off, I felt ready to create possibilities for realizing my dream of a soul-hearted partnership with myself first and then with a beloved partner.

The conscious awareness that we can cocreate our own possibilities for a fully realized partnership with ourselves as the basis for an inspiring and fulfilling partnership with another person became the genesis of *Soul-Hearted Partnership: Creating the Ultimate Experience of Love, Passion, and Intimacy*. The spiritual principles I discuss in the book have been the foundation for my personal transformation and the fulfilling relationships I've cocreated since that pivotal moment. Regardless of one's life circumstances, it is always possible to cultivate a fulfilling partnership because the power to do so resides within ourselves rather than in other people or external situations. It is my hope that this book, which encourages active participation in the form of exercises and journaling, will guide others to create the necessary conditions for a fully realized relationship with themselves and a soul-hearted partnership with others.

# Introduction

*I*N OUR CULTURE, creating healthy, passionate, and loving relationships is one of the most widely discussed topics. We constantly read about it in the tabloids and see it modeled on television and in the movies. Workshops are packed with people wanting to improve every aspect of their relationships, while singles bars, dating clubs, and Internet classified ads focusing on romance abound.

Yet despite all the attention relationships receive in today's world, our perception of them is often influenced by our childhood experiences. Most of us remember as children having fairy tales read to us, such as *Cinderella, Sleeping Beauty,* or *Snow White.* Even though each story had different characters and plots, they all led us to the same conclusion—the hero and heroine lived happily ever after—leaving us with the impression that dreams of perfect relationships come true.

As children we clearly envisioned our dreams, never doubting our innate power to fulfill our human potential and attain happy relationships. Even if we didn't understand how the process worked, we felt its truth through our open hearts, regardless of our external circumstances. Open and optimistic, we had not yet acquired the adult mindsets and beliefs that inhibit our ability to channel this creative energy positively and productively.

In contrast, as adults, because of disillusioning experiences or societal beliefs and expectations, most of us are convinced that living happily ever after exists in movies and fiction but rarely in real life. Despite the allure of such updated fairy tales as *My Fair Lady, Pretty Woman, Under the Tuscan Sun, Ever After, Sleepless in Seattle,* and *An Affair to Remember,* we have stifled our instinctive ability to surmount all obstacles and make our dreams a reality. Many of us may not even believe that we are in charge of our destiny. Unfortunately, the mind's control is so great that merely by thinking that we have lost our ability to manifest our dreams we undermine our creative power to make them come true.

We can only have soul-hearted partnerships, however, upon realizing our natural ability to tap this energy source, manifest the fullest expression of ourselves, and share this expanded experience of life in relationships connected on all levels—physically, mentally, emotionally, and spiritually. What I call "soul-hearted" is a sustained flow of energy passing from our source through our heart center, enabling us to have a soul-connected relationship first with ourselves and then, through an intertwining of these energies, with another person. This energetically charged love, passion, and intimacy both supports the soul progression of each individual and, when consciously channeled into the partnership, contributes to an amazing life together.

Much has been written on the challenges of relationships due to gender differences, typified perhaps by the bestseller *Men Are from Mars, Women Are from Venus*. Looking at gender differences is helpful when assessing the broad challenges of individuals within relationships. Men may be more animalistic and geared toward conquest, so to have a fulfilling relationship at a deeper spiritual level they have to grow beyond wanting to control a partner. In contrast, women tend to lose their own identity in relationships while focusing on their partner or family—a phenomenon that exists even among those who also have a career. They struggle to keep in mind that they are whole and worthwhile beings apart from their partner or children, especially since historically they have often been made to think their role in relationships is subsidiary. Consequently, to have a fulfilling relationship at a deeper spiritual level women need to grow beyond any perception of themselves as second-class citizens. And although some of these gender differences seem to be verified by brain research and supported by social programming, I propose we can move beyond our gender-related behavioral differences to an intertwining of masculine and feminine energies expressed individually and as a couple.

The flow of energy I associate with soul-hearted relationships transcends categories of male or female, becoming greater than the energy of the involved individuals. This energetic dynamic differs significantly from former models of relationship, such as husband and wife or partners, and can occur in all types of relationships, including friendships in which individuals have a soul connection with another person. As a result, this flow of energy can keep expanding in various aspects of our lives until our whole life experience becomes characterized by it—becomes soul-hearted.

So it is that soul-hearted relationships result not from intersecting events, as in fate or chance, but from drawing on an energy source we can channel to expand conscious awareness and undergo personal transformation. In becoming a conduit for this energy source, we can direct it to fashion the life we desire. Expressing this energy through our hearts allows us to overcome negative mindsets, beliefs, and behavioral patterns; dissolve old identity structures; and increase the happiness and fulfillment in our lives. Channeling this energy proactively and not making our happiness dependent on external circumstances leads to an abundance of all that is good.

When we unequivocally trust ourselves to draw on this divine energy source, we begin to see that we create our own reality. Trusting our connection to this source of creation ignites our intentions, which in turn opens us to see more possibilities and make quality choices that will benefit us in the future.

Taking charge of our destiny in this way requires us to nurture and sustain a more conscious relationship with ourselves by becoming aware of and accountable for everything in our lives—every thought, feeling, and choice we make. Being responsible for ourselves means becoming aware of our negative perceptions, the dynamics of current relationships, and our prospects for the future. The intrinsic power to realize our dreams allows us not only to believe again in the miracle of happily-ever-after outcomes but to go beyond passively waiting for the fairy tale ending and have a more proactive relationship with our destiny. The fairy tale scenario often depends on the expectation of something happening and then waiting for it to happen, like Sleeping Beauty waiting for her prince to rescue her from slumber. In contrast, going beyond such fairy tale scenarios means using our innate power to manifest our dreams, as well as choosing to live fully expressed in every moment, no matter what is happening in our lives. It is up to *us* to fulfill our potential as individuals and then attract, develop, and sustain the most inspiring and fulfilling relationships possible.

To begin this process it is important to more fully understand why most people have difficulty realizing their dreams and establishing fully realized relationships. Over the years, I have listened to many people searching for answers to the questions "How did I lose myself and my dreams?" and "How did I forget that I have the innate power to create my dreams?" My response to them is that they deferred listening to their own inner voice and instead listened to the voices of others, absorbing external programming. Family, friends, and society all help to program us with the message that to achieve real happiness we must make sacrifices—including compromising our true selves.

At times, nearly everyone has been taught to believe that their dreams, the proverbial pink bubble, were unattainable. Well-meaning parents, friends, and teachers reprimanded them when they daydreamed or attempted to share their visions. Being chastised when they had their head in the clouds and lectured that life was too serious to waste in fantasizing about impossible dreams, they struggled to fit in, yielded to the opinions of others, and dismissed their dreams.

As for the trouble we have establishing fully realized relationships, because of neediness and lack of self-esteem we often seek someone to complete or guide us. Such behavior is reinforced by society's frequent message that we are nobody unless we have somebody—a notion derived from the outdated expectation that each person in any relationship gives 50 percent. The inherent problem with this idea is that if each partner thinks the other will pick up the remaining 50 percent of energy investment in the relationship, neither one is operating at full throttle and thus the relationship is never truly complete.

Programmed with such negative mindsets, and rarely seeing healthy and fulfilling relationships modeled outside the imaginative world of cinema or books, we persuade ourselves that our destiny comes from external events, not the flow of energy through our hearts. And when we fail to realize our dreams and experience successive disappointing relationships, we convince ourselves that this is "as good as it gets." We settle for mediocrity for ourselves because we are unable to imagine more fulfilling relationships, let alone manifest our intention of a fully realized relationship with a partner.

A good way to counteract this trend is to recognize that in dismissing our dreams we disregard our natural ability to fully express ourselves. Like Snow White being enticed to take a bite from the poisoned apple, we become seduced by the spell of lethal messages reinforcing our feelings of powerlessness and tune out the voice of spirit speaking through the heart, which urges us to dream. It takes a loving, trusting relationship with ourselves to avoid succumbing to this spell so that we remain awake and inspired to follow our heart's desires. Not following the voice of spirit speaking through our heart is life's ultimate compromise. In disconnecting from our spiritual source and losing the true foundation for creating the life we most desire, we not only forfeit our dreams but perpetuate unhealthy and unfulfilling relationships, having settled for a lifetime of routine experiences.

But unlike protagonists in fairy tales or movies who must overcome obstacles, we do not have to trudge through life's lessons to realize our dreams or attain fulfilling relationships. The only dragons we need to slay are the negative mindsets that stand between us and our future prospects. Releasing our negative mindsets begins with supplanting beliefs such as "My dreams are pure fantasy" and "This is the best relationship I'll ever have" with affirmations such as "I can make my dreams come true" and "I can have the best relationships possible." Next, we can listen to the voice of spirit speaking through our heart, telling us that we are the creators of our own reality. Then, feeling completely free to dream without inhibition, we can imagine our ideal life without limitations. In seeing life from this perspective, we open ourselves to new possibilities and ways to manifest them through our intentions.

The spiritual principles presented in *Soul-Hearted Partnership: Creating the Ultimate Experience of Love, Passion, and Intimacy* form a blueprint for first developing a fully realized relationship with ourselves, and then sharing an inspiring and fulfilling relationship with another person. Being happy with ourselves, even when alone, is the basis for being truly happy with someone else. So, before we can enter into such a relationship with another individual, we need to be consciously in touch with our true being. For purposes of this book, I have fine-tuned the spiritual principles recommended for a soul-hearted partnership during workshops, retreats, and thousands of individual consultations so that they can easily be incorporated into everyday life. By consistently using these principles, you not only sustain a soul-hearted partnership with yourself but also cocreate such a relationship with others, including a beloved partner who desires to share a more enriching life with you. Using examples of experiences in my own life and those of clients, this book also describes circumstances that both undermine and foster the development of soul-hearted partnerships.

Part I focuses on initiating and sustaining a fully realized relationship with yourself to attain a personal experience of soul-hearted partnership. The principles of expanding and using conscious awareness, opening your heart, recognizing and releasing patterns and unresolved grievances, cocreating your reality by manifesting intentions, and sustaining a soul-hearted partnership with yourself are discussed as guidelines for personal transformation.

Expanding and using conscious awareness involves establishing and trusting your connection to your spiritual source, being open to new information that adds to awareness of yourself and the world, and being a conscious observer of your experience so you can better respond to life's circumstances by acting on the inner knowledge you receive.

Opening your heart entails self-love as the prerequisite for soul-hearted partnership, learning to listen to the voice of spirit speaking through your heart and guiding you, and becoming your own loving coach.

Recognizing and releasing patterns, including unfulfilling relationships, paves the way for unblocking energy that prevents the experience of fulfillment in situations and relationships. This allows you to access and eliminate any mindset or belief that no longer serves you so you can focus on choices that open your heart and allow you to see new possibilities.

Cocreating your reality is about directing the flow of positive energy to make the discerning choices that manifest your intentions, resulting in a fully realized partnership with yourself and preparing the way for making your dreams a reality.

Sustaining soul-hearted partnership with yourself involves maintaining trust in yourself and your connection to source, building an energetic support team, and preparing for an eventual soul-hearted partnership with another person.

Part II reveals ways to apply these spiritual principles for cocreating and sustaining a soul-hearted partnership through the exchange of unconditional love, absolute trust, open and clear communications, and the experience of intimacy on all levels. It shows why you may have settled for unsatisfying relationships in the past and demonstrates how to develop and maintain inspired and fulfilling relationships now. It also presents soul-hearted partnership, in which each partner is complete and not just an extension of the other, as more than the sum of the individuals involved, resulting in a combined balance of 100/100/100 percent of the energies of each partner and of the couple together to form an unparalleled relationship.

Throughout the book, each chapter concludes with suggestions for practicing the featured principles in daily life. Practice them for as long as you wish, returning to them selectively as needed.

Falling in love is one thing; establishing and sustaining a soul-hearted partnership is quite another. May the material in this book help you direct your personal power to cocreate the life you have always wanted.

# PART I

# The Personal Experience
# of Soul-Hearted Partnership

# Chapter One
## EXPANDING AND USING CONSCIOUS AWARENESS

"There are only two ways to live your life. One is as though nothing is a miracle. The other is as though everything is a miracle."
— ALBERT EINSTEIN

*B*EFORE WE CAN ENTER INTO SOUL-HEARTED RELATIONSHIP with another individual, we need to develop a fully realized relationship with ourselves so we can operate in the world from our true being as an unequivocally responsible individual. To engage in this personal experience of soul-hearted partnership, we must first manifest the intention to get in touch with the core of our being. There is much confusion between the concepts of ego, personality, identity, and the core of our being. At the physical level, we can only experience individuality. At the soul level, however, we can experience a more undifferentiated pure essence—a flow of energy without the distinctions of ego, personality, and identity. In this state, we are in touch with the core of our being and aware of ourselves as manifestations of the source of creation. This flow of energy is expressed in everyday life as a soul-hearted relationship with ourselves.

The intention to cultivate a soul-hearted relationship with ourselves is a catalyst for expanding conscious awareness, resulting in clearer thinking, enhanced creativity, more positive energy flow, and ultimately forming the foundation for self-realization. This intention alone leads to a positive shift in our perspective on life, opens us to spiritual development, and guides us to express our fullest potential.

### The Function of Conscious Awareness
Conscious awareness is our intuitive ability to tune in to spiritual information that expands our understanding of ourselves and our circumstances,

providing us with a broader perspective from which to make better life choices. It involves simultaneously seeing ourselves from our heads and our hearts, unlike the tendency most people have of experiencing internal conflict between their intellect and their feelings, resulting in emotional distress. Like Hansel and Gretel walking through the enchanted forest, conscious awareness gives us spiritual breadcrumbs to guide us—clues that direct us on our soul's journey. Following these spiritual guideposts bypasses logical thinking and awakens an instantaneous inner knowing through the heart. You may have experienced conscious awareness as a feeling of "aha" or as a moment of sudden clarity when everything comes into focus as if through a telescope.

By expanding and using conscious awareness, we can access a greater wealth of information to support our spiritual growth and well-being and to develop better relationships. In doing this we begin to shift from viewing things simply in physical terms to seeing why things happen from a spiritual perspective. We are then equipped to act from the core of our being and engage in the personal experience of soul-hearted partnership.

Marion Zimmer Bradley's *Mists of Avalon* provides a good illustration of conscious awareness. In it, Avalon, an island that exists behind veils of what appear to be impenetrable mists, symbolizes a mystical world beyond the mere physical world seen with our eyes, a world that, as children, we sensed with wonder. To access this world, people must see with the eyes of their heart, which shifts their perception outside the realm of physicality and expands their conscious awareness. As Antoine de Saint-Exupéry states in *The Little Prince*, "It is only with the heart that one can see rightly; what is essential is invisible to the eye."[1]

According to both ancient mysticism and modern philosophical thought, the secret to experiencing conscious awareness is to free ourselves from the ego, a brain-induced, time-oriented self-projection. In this unhindered and unlimited state, we feel connected no longer to our material surroundings but rather to a flowing, intelligent energy source, realizing that although we appear as solid matter on a physical level, we are actually intersecting energy fields, each one formless, vibrating, and containing all information in the universe. This state allows us to see ourselves as an unfolding manifestation of the source of all being—God, divine intelligence, higher power, or whatever one chooses to call it. From this perspective of expanded conscious awareness, we become aware of valuable information in the form of hunches, gut feelings, extrasensory perceptions, or divine synchronicities that provide us with a perspective extending beyond our day-to-day preoccupations so we can make better choices for a more fulfilling life.

Ways in which conscious awareness helps us override logic and tune in to psychic or intuitive abilities are illustrated by the following examples. Suppose you are driving to meet your father, doubting the wisdom of such an encounter, then see a sign that reads, "Fathers matter." Or perhaps you have a strong desire to call a friend whom you have not seen in a while, and suddenly your friend phones you or you run into her at the grocery store. Or you may be pondering a problem and out of the blue an enlightened solution to it pops into your mind. An example from my personal life occurred when I was telling a friend about a financial decision I had made for my daughter Alex's college fund based on the recommendation of my financial planner, who called at that moment wanting to discuss new investment options.

I am often asked for reassurance about the significance of such signs by people who feel devoid of spiritual guidance in their lives. They ask because they do not know how to trust the spiritual information coming through the heart. Instead of attuning to their hearts, they hold on to a particular mindset or belief dictating that events in their lives should follow a logical order and thus fail to recognize the significance of such clues. Or if they do recognize the importance of these clues they are often afraid to act on them, seeing the consequences as too challenging to the status quo. Yet never are we guided to expand ourselves spiritually beyond our ability at any given moment.

To more actively access conscious awareness, we can continually scan and absorb information with our senses. As we willingly become more open, our sensory perceptions become clearer and we become more receptive to spiritual clues. We know we are receiving such clues when we feel a rush of energy that makes our hair stand on end, gives us goose bumps, causes us to feel a tingling sensation, a buzzing, or simply a warming or subtle tension in parts of the body. Many people acknowledge these experiences with comments such as "I can sense it in my body," "I can feel it in my bones," or "The answer is right on the tip of my tongue." When I work with clients, I often receive information about them in the form of physical sensations in my body, intuitive feelings, and sharpened visual perceptions.

Like a spiritual compass or global positioning system, conscious awareness assists us in navigating the events in our lives. Using it can feel like being in a hovercraft supported by a cushion of air blowing downward, with the lift of our spirit creating a perspective for us that takes in the circumstances of our lives from three hundred and sixty degrees. Or it can feel like flying in an airplane and viewing the myriad of details on the ground below. As such, conscious awareness assists us in moving outside of whatever is happening in our lives so we can assess situations with detachment. Every experience we have, no matter how trivial—a surly driver who cuts us off in traffic, a waiter who will not look our way, the unexpected loss of a close relationship, or a rainstorm that drenches us to the bone—can then be viewed through our conscious awareness as something wonderful, humorous, or simply an opportunity to learn more about ourselves. From this inspired vantage point, we are free to float in the space of all possibilities without being attached to a particular outcome and thus able to make enlightened choices capable of transforming our lives. Although seeing your life from such a perspective may be initially disorienting because it shifts your perception of things, using conscious awareness is actually an innate skill requiring only minimal practice.

In *Anatomy of the Spirit*, medical intuitive Carolyn Myss defines this type of enlightened state as "symbolic sight, the ability to use your intuition to interpret the power symbols in your life."[2] Transformational seer Bryan Christopher refers to such an experience as "fluid awareness or seeing, and a level of spiritual support that constantly can be tapped, looked at, and utilized in real life."[3]

The following story illustrates how to expand and use conscious awareness to support self-realization. Several weeks after my husband Doug and I became engaged, we were having a quiet dinner at one of our favorite Italian restaurants when we began conversing about our future wedding plans. Doug was in a "let's wait and see" mode, while I felt a strong need to immediately set a date for our wedding. As he evaded my attempts to set a date, I sensed tension in my diaphragm and a shortness of breath, indicating anxiety. My physical reaction cued me to pause, release the tension by breathing deeply, and listen to my heart to gain an understanding of the new information I was being guided to see.

At that moment, I also observed our interaction from the perspective of expanded conscious awareness, as if I were simultaneously acting in and directing a movie. On the one hand, my brain-induced ego made me feel like an actor focusing on scripted lines relating to my need to control the situation due to my pattern of abandonment and Doug's pattern of avoidance. I wanted to set the wedding date so I could assuage my fear that he would abandon our relationship if I didn't "close the deal" soon. On the other hand, my expanded conscious awareness allowed me to experience a connection to a divine energy source guiding me to see that I would never be alone, could let go of fear, and stop investing in a particular outcome. After seeing the situation from this vantage point, instead of overreacting to Doug's comment I was able to maintain a healthy detachment from the situation, release my reaction, and enjoy the rest of the evening without any agenda. As a result, Doug sensed the shift in my attitude and we were able to share our vision of the future together from a broader perspective not based on fear or need. This experience validated that I could trust myself and the partnership I was cocreating with Doug, and thus achieve greater intimacy with him.

We can also use this valuable tool of conscious awareness to illuminate which negative thoughts, feelings, and behavioral patterns are inhibiting our ability to establish a soul-hearted partnership with ourselves and others. When we evaluate past situations from such a perspective, we are using hindsight that eventually leads to insight. Hindsight, which confers the equivalent of 20/20 vision, helps us interpret the past according to the more expansive perspective of the present; it is a way of using conscious awareness after the fact to evaluate information already stored in the brain. This affords us increased insight on both past and present experiences so that we can make positive choices in the future.

As we develop a more expansive view of ourselves, we discover how to stay clear of the web of daily minutia that can entangle us, while tapping into the flow of spiritual information guiding us. It is our birthright as human beings to have direct access to this information in order to serve as a channel through which it flows. As we connect with a divine source for guidance and become a conduit of pure energy and spiritual information, it becomes increasingly possible to create positive transformation in all aspects of our lives.

### Trusting Our Connection to Source

Creating a more fulfilling life requires absolute trust in our connection to source. We have the power to create either positively by trusting our connection to source or negatively by surrendering to our fear-based patterns. Fortunately, we can shift from the fear-based message that we are powerless over our lives to the affirmation that we are the creators of our own reality, making us more capable of manifesting positive outcomes.

In this discussion, source means the origin of pure energy that flows through each of us—also known as light energy, higher power, universal energy, divine intelligence, or God, depending on one's point of view. Ultimately, light energy expressed through our hearts radiates unconditional love. Light energy is the essence of all that exists, and when we access it we are able to fully express our being. Although formless, it has energetic power to affect physical entities, manifest intentions, and provide spiritual information.

Bryan Christopher describes light energy as the source of all we are and came to be, suggesting we are all part of a vast expanse of illuminating energy. As pure energy, light moves through space, is pulled into an energy field called gravity, and attracts matter. This energetic attraction becomes thought, which informs the body, and then information, which guides us to speak, feel, or act, and is our direct link to our soul. Channeled through us, this light energy transforms us into creational beings capable of manifesting intentions to cocreate our reality. When we trust our connection to source and are aware of this creative energy from source flowing through us, we see that we are able to channel it to support the fullest expression of ourselves and manifest our dreams. Knowing that we are conduits for this energy helps keep us from being negatively affected by events in life and aids us in overcoming our fear-based patterns and manifesting our intentions. And in trusting our connection to source we become our own soul mate, at which point we discover that we are complete within ourselves and begin to express our fullest soul potential. To a greater extent, this connection with ourselves and with source becomes the foundation on which we can establish and sustain a healthy relationship with another person.

Unfortunately, many people lack absolute trust in their connection to this divine energy source and thus live in fear. Perceiving everyone as a potential enemy and everything as disaster in the making, they continually check the stock market or current value of their home to see if they are financially secure; they worry about wrinkles or physical symptoms, thinking they may be ill or growing old; they remain in unhealthy relationships to avoid being alone; they maintain social connections to make sure they belong; they try to secure their job by working for a promotion; or they feel anxious when anything threatens the status quo or offers an opportunity for change. Consequently, they live in a guarded state, with locks on their hearts as well as their doors to avoid getting hurt or feeling unloved. Since they feel separated from their own vital being, it is no wonder they often have difficulty developing healthy and fulfilling relationships.

Underlying these types of behaviors is often a fear of death, which influences all of our choices. We try to control and hold on to everything in our possession to reassure ourselves that we physically exist. While we may mentally understand that change is a constant, when people we love die, or we lose our job, or a close relationship ends, we panic instead of releasing the past so that we can embrace our future. Unfortunately, this inability to accept change and release the past blocks the flow of energy we need to progress on our soul's path and produce a meaningful partnership with ourselves and others.

Establishing absolute trust in our connection to source is a key for manifesting a more rewarding life based on internal security. Even though we may often feel like we are operating without a safety net, our connection to source is in fact our safety net. In trusting this connection we realize that even though we are ultimately alone in the world, we should not feel insecure because we are not separate from the rest of humanity and have the resource of spiritual information at our disposal. Although people often allow their life experiences to reinforce a sense of spiritual disconnection, which accounts for many of humanity's problems, such alienation interferes with having the healthy relationships we want in our lives since it fuels an obsessive need to be physically and emotionally attached to people for the wrong reasons; this attachment frequently results in the breakdown of relationships and intensified feelings of alienation. Embracing that we are the embodiment of unconditional love and light is the key to expanding beyond feelings of alienation that prevent us from expressing ourselves as fully as possible.

Albert Einstein affirms the value of seeing life in this broader context of connection with source: "A human being is a part of a whole, called by us, universe; a part limited by time and space. He experiences himself, his thoughts and feelings as something separated from the rest—a kind of optical illusion of his consciousness. This delusion is a kind of prison for us, restricting us to our personal desires and to affection for a few persons nearest us. Our task must be to free ourselves from this prison by widening our circle of compassion to embrace all living creatures and the whole of nature in its beauty. Nobody is able to achieve this completely, but striving for such achievement is, in itself, a part of the liberation and a foundation for inner security."[4]

In essence, trusting our connection to source governs how we perceive and respond to all challenges in life. It affords us the personal power to express unconditional love, flow with the stream of external events, and transcend difficult circumstances. For example, with such trust we can embrace every situation not as a source of fear or upset but as an opportunity for growth even when it unravels the fabric of our lives, such as losing a job, ending a relationship, suffering from an illness, or grieving the loss of a loved one. Directing this energy positively in every situation allows us to live beyond negative mindsets, beliefs, and behavioral patterns that cause us to second-guess ourselves. Like any personal training routine, with sustained practice we then build confidence and open to new possibilities.

Trusting ourselves in connection to source enables us to consistently make intentions that align with our core being. Like Sleeping Beauty, we must awaken from our spellbound slumber to live purposefully, in accord with who we truly are. As we embrace the beauty of our being, we generate our own powerful spell and feel motivated to live every aspect of our lives as a miracle.

### Becoming Conscious Observers of Our Experience

Becoming conscious observers of our experience—our thoughts, feelings, behavioral patterns, and life circumstances—allows us to witness our lives from a healthy detached perspective and assess any situation from a broad viewpoint. This ability is an outgrowth of an expanded conscious awareness that becomes activated when we trust our connection to source. Like operating the zoom lens of a camera, we can pull ourselves away from any experience to access a more spiritually relevant point of view.

Consciously observing our experience from an objective, expanded viewpoint helps us gain perspective on and disengage from negative reactions such as blaming, attacking, or resisting others when we feel angry or irritable. Invariably, no one in the outside world has directly caused our discomfort. In fact, the brain, like a camera, has filtered lenses through which we perceive external circumstances. The filters, which originate in past experiences, alter how we see and interpret new information. Thus in interacting with someone for the first time, our filtered lenses may distort our perception of them and cause us to react negatively.

In many cases, we may discover that we are not angry at the person but rather at the information we are receiving about ourselves—the particular mindset, belief, or behavioral pattern triggered by the encounter. In other words, though at first it may feel like we want to kill the messenger what we really want to eliminate is the message. In *Rising Out of Chaos*, Simon Peter Fuller writes, "What angers us in another person is more often than not an unhealed aspect of ourselves. If we had already resolved that particular issue, we would not be irritated by its reflection back to us."[5]

In such situations, there are several things we can do to uncover the unresolved issue demanding our attention and to better control our reaction. First, to relate a reaction to an unresolved issue, it is helpful to ask ourselves: "What physical, mental, or emotional sensations am I experiencing right now?" "What is this person or situation showing me about my own mindsets, beliefs, or behavioral patterns?" "Are there any I need to identify and release?"

Second, to better control a reaction, we can walk out of the room, set the phone down, or write a response in a letter or e-mail to send later. When we allow the reaction to happen without directing it to a person, it will usually dissipate. For example, in martial arts training, students learn to move toward or sidestep rather than resisting an attacker's advances so the negative energy then ricochets back in their direction. Likewise, when we move toward what we are resisting we disperse the negative energy surrounding the issue.

Third, in general we can take purposeful breaks during the day to assess and overcome reactions from encounters with others. Paying attention to discomfort or tension in the body when in potentially uncomfortable situations, listening to the information being received, and identifying, or flagging, negative patterns can aid in toning down reactions.

Finally, separating our patterned reactions from someone else's gives us the healthy distance needed to avoid taking theirs personally or blaming them for ours, while staying lovingly connected and responsive. It helps to envision the person going through their own self-discovery that likely has nothing to do with us. This form of compassionate detachment increases our ability to influence difficult situations with positive energy. In choosing to respond, rather than react by taking the person's issues to heart, we give the individual loving space in which to examine the source of their own reactions and, subsequently, release them. When we provide another person with the opportunity to release fear-based negative patterns, we open doors for better interactions in the future.

My therapeutic work with my client Chris illustrates how resistance, discomfort, or other negative reactions provide information about unresolved issues. For most of his life, Chris had been tormented by anxiety about being able to provide for his family. Recently, he had been concerned about facing possible financial ruin because of a bad real estate deal. His feelings of insecurity haunted him at night as he paced through his house while his family slept, asking himself, "Why am I allowing fear and anxiety to run my life?"

Over several sessions, I showed Chris how to recognize physical, mental, and emotional reactions that "flag" unresolved issues. First, I assisted him in seeing that his anxiety was alerting him to negative mindsets and beliefs stemming from a lack of trust in himself and his connection to source that would allow him to produce an abundant life. In his mind, "I don't have enough" translated to "I'm not enough." This negative mentality was instigating a self-destructive pattern of scarcity, fueling his need to control everything in his life and perpetuating his role as a victim of circumstances.

Then I guided him to observe his experience, especially in uncomfortable situations, and ask himself, "What is this irritability, annoyance, or anxiety telling me about my behavioral patterns?" As a result, he began to see how, if left unaddressed, his patterns would continue to cause him anxiety and undermine his sense of well-being. He also saw how his anxious reactions could assist him in realizing that he was stuck in a fear-based pattern and needed to move past it.

I have taught my clients to use various tools in dealing with circumstances that cause irritation or anxiety. One helpful tool is giving ourselves "permission to pause" in any situation that arouses a physical, mental, or emotional reaction, thus providing time to gain detachment. After pushing the pause button, we can listen to our heart rather than react from our fear-based mentality, avoid knee-jerk reactions, and consciously observe the situation from a more expansive perspective. Taking such a purposeful break affords us the opportunity to explore the root of negative mindsets, beliefs, and the self-destructive patterns they trigger. Examining which patterns have surfaced allows us to override their influence and tune in to spiritual information flowing through the heart, which is more aligned with our true being. We can also reframe our anxiety or irritation, viewing it as a signal that something new is coming our way.

Another tool for countering reactivity is using a visual cue, such as a stop sign, comma, or pause button. Envisioning such a cue, or having it displayed near a phone or desk, or on a computer screen, where situations may arise that provoke resistance, can be an automatic reminder to stop, release a reaction, and then respond consciously.

Finally, watching yourself as if in slow motion will give you more time to become aware of your thoughts and emotions, and ultimately to release reactions. This occurs because slowing our pace moves us into a present-oriented state unattached to prior irritations or anxiety. It is difficult to release reactions when, on an emotional scale of one to ten, you have already moved to a nine or ten.

Being a conscious observer of our experience and learning to disengage from reactions allows us to become more proactive instead of reactive, shifting our energy from negative to positive. As a result, we can begin viewing difficult circumstances as opportunities to transform our lives.

**Miracles occur when we expand and use our conscious awareness and subsequently sustain a flow of positive energy no matter what the circum-**

stances. Expanding and using our conscious awareness, we witness the core of our being from a viewpoint determined by the integration of head and heart perspectives. Such integration offers us insight about ourselves and our relationships, as well as the opportunity to be a creative channel for its energy to flow through us and to manifest positive outcomes. This is living as though everything is a miracle.

PRACTICING THE PRINCIPLES IN CHAPTER ONE

1. *Practice expanding your conscious awareness.* Use the visual images of being in a hovercraft gliding over water or aloft in an airplane looking at the ground as a way to view your life's circumstances from a broader, more spiritual perspective. Begin by viewing a particular situation from this new vantage point. With practice, you will be able to move beyond the limitations of any circumstance and perceive the events in your life as opportunities for self-healing and spiritual growth.

2. *Use your conscious awareness on a daily basis.* Maintain a reflective or meditative attitude as you move through your day. Pay attention to moments of sudden clarity and synchronicities that occur when you least expect them. Acknowledge the things that seem to happen for a reason; recognize the circumstances without judging them as good or bad. Perceive every interaction or condition as an opportunity for personal transformation.

3. *Engage in activities that expand your conscious awareness, especially when you feel bogged down in challenging circumstances.* Spend time in nature, meditate, or engage in therapy, energy work, yoga, massage, or acupuncture to help release any tension, toxicity, or constriction and open you to the flow of positive energy.

4. *Cleanse your energetic field by showering whenever you have been in a toxic physical or emotional environment.* Use water, which can be seen as liquid light energy, for cleansing your energetic field after a stressful day or difficult interaction to maintain a constant flow of positive energy through your body.

5. *Affirm your trust in your connection to source.* See yourself as a conduit of light energy, and sustain a continuous flow of divine energy through your heart. Be aware of choices coming through this channel for manifesting your intentions, and follow through on creative ideas and projects.

6. *Trust and affirm your being.* Use the following positive affirmations for awakening your divine ability to transform your life: "I express my fullest self so others can benefit," "I sow seeds of light wherever I go, leaving it a better place for having been there," "I trust that I am the cocreator of my life," "I embody light and love," "I know and trust who I am," and "I celebrate life, express unconditional love, and sustain my well-being."

7. *Practice being a conscious observer of your experience.* Observe your interactions and conditions from a broader, more detached perspective, paying attention to any cues signaling that negative mindsets, beliefs, or patterns may be inhibiting positive life developments. Tune in to your reactions and, from an expanded viewpoint, see each one as an opportunity to address an unresolved issue likely to otherwise limit your possibilities. Also explore any discomfort suggesting that an unresolved issue may have surfaced.

8. *Practice being a conscious observer of your sensations.* Observe where your body holds tension or pain, then ask yourself, "What is going on inside me at this moment?" "Why am I feeling sensations here?" and "What information am I being given?" Accept that your body will always give you a true indication of your thoughts, feelings, and patterns.

9. *Give yourself permission to pause.* Take time out to pay attention to reactions you may be having to people and circumstances. Then explore the implications through journaling or talking to a trusted partner, friend, or therapist. Routinely visualize a stop sign or a comma to pause and evaluate your reactions. Practice remaining open to new information, ideas, and points of view.

# Chapter Two
## Opening the Heart

"Nobody has ever measured, not even poets,
how much the heart can hold."
—WILLIAM BLAKE

Opening the heart unlocks the door to unconditional love and expression of the light within us. When we open our hearts and expand our consciousness, we receive spiritual information about who we are and our soul's progression. At the same time, a light force signaling unconditional love moves through us as we go about our day-to-day lives.

Given the turmoil in today's world, it is crucial to focus on the power of the heart. Its expression of unconditional love can be either universal, pertaining to everyone and everything, or relative, directed to one person or thing. Examples of expressing universal love are "I love people and want peace and harmony in the world" and "I send love and light to everyone and see everything as love." Examples of expressing relative love are "I love my job," "I love you," and "I love me." Expressing unconditional love that incorporates both universal and relative love expands our consciousness beyond the limits of our minds and conditions of the physical world, and unleashes the most powerful source of energy on earth.

### Self-Love As the Prerequisite for Soul-Hearted Love

Entering a soul-hearted partnership with another person requires us to first open our hearts and unconditionally love ourselves. When we love ourselves, we become our own safe haven, where we feel free to fully express who we are and realize our dreams. Opening our hearts so we can love ourselves without qualification is the foundation for developing a soul-hearted partnership with another, characterized by the mutual expression of unconditional love.

As psychoanalyst and philosopher Eric Fromm states in *The Art of Loving*, "What matters in relation to love is the faith in one's own love; in its ability to produce love in others. We are only capable of knowing and caring for the other if we are also capable of understanding, caring, and knowing ourselves."[1] Stated differently, to experience soul-hearted love, we must first embody genuine love.

Difficulty with loving ourselves directly impacts the thoughts and feelings we have, the choices we make, the relationships we select, and how we perceive and react to every life situation. Feelings that we are unlovable occur due to our early childhood environment and as a result of our hearts disconnecting from our true being and our source. When we close off our hearts, we are more likely to take things personally, and then blame or attack others—a reaction that follows because we have automatically assumed that we are unlovable, not good enough, or there is something wrong with us.

The blocked unconditional love of ourselves ultimately threatens the expression of unconditional love in our relationships. We have all witnessed couples giving each other a broken heart on a necklace as a symbol of their love. Although wearing this symbol may be endearing, it implies that the only way we can be complete is with our "missing half." Since we cannot have a fulfilling relationship unless we feel complete in and love ourselves unconditionally, however, it is not surprising that many people even with their "other half" still feel incomplete.

In contrast, self-love leads to acceptance of the intrinsically spiritual nature of our being. Deeper than our patterns and structured identity is our true being—our sense of aliveness and authentic relatedness. We can experience this aspect of being with a child, friend, partner, coworker, stranger, or even a dog by opening our hearts, which allows unconditional love to flow through us. Through heart connections with others, we see that we are no longer separate but rather one in the collective flow of unconditional love.

With practice, we can master the art of loving and self-loving. My client Kathy's self-loving troubles began in early childhood when her mother became ill with Huntington's disease, a degenerative neurological disorder. During one of our sessions, Kathy recalled an experience at age eight of being in a school play, wearing a frilly pink princess costume her grandmother had made for her, and feeling her heart sink when she realized that her mother wasn't in the audience. Despite her deep disappointment, she knew the show must go on.

With this mantra in mind, Kathy tried to always do everything right and be the good girl so that her mother would love her and not abandon her. Despite her best efforts, when Kathy was ten her father placed her mother in a residential assisted living facility. She remembered thinking to herself, "If only I had done more or been better, my mother would have never left me." Not prepared for this abrupt separation and taking her mother's absence personally, Kathy closed her heart so that she could suppress her painful loss.

A year later her father divorced her mother and remarried without first sharing the news with Kathy. When her new stepmother came to live with them and started making derogatory comments about her mother, instead of expressing her feelings Kathy chose not to rock the boat. Deep down, she was terrified to talk to anyone about her mother or the disease because she knew she was at risk for it as well and in her world of magical thinking, she assumed that if she didn't talk about it, it wouldn't happen to her. As a result, over the next few years Kathy's rage turned inward and she became severely depressed then anorexic. In her own way, she had mounted a silent protest against the pressure to be a "nice girl" who accepted peace at all costs.

In the fall of her sophomore year in college, Kathy's mother died in a nursing home, and Kathy's painful cry for help finally got the attention of her family. After watching her shrink before their eyes, they could no longer ignore her plea for love.

With support from me, her grandmother, and friends, Kathy gradually discovered how to love herself and forgive her past. I guided her through the grieving process, which allowed her to open her heart. She began to see that she could put her disappointment about the limitations of her parents' love in perspective and, each time she thought of them, focus energy through her heart and forgive them. The more she did this, the more she opened her heart and was able to channel unconditional love as compassion. Seeing herself in a positive light made it easier for her to love herself, receive love, and feel spiritually connected.

The key to self-love is knowing and accepting your true being. The first step begins with what John Welwood, psychotherapist and teacher, refers to in *Perfect Love, Imperfect Relationships*, as "letting yourself have your own experience." He goes on to say, "If you can let your experience happen, it will release its knots and unfold, leading to a deeper, more grounded experience of yourself."[2]

At the same time, we have to trust that our experience is unique and valuable. Sharing it with others may cause us to think it is not unique, but in fact no one else can ever have our experience. Accepting it as valuable can be especially challenging for those of us who are accustomed to ignoring, avoiding, or distracting ourselves from personal experiences.

Initiating self-love by accepting our true being requires paying attention to whatever is going on at any given moment, opening the heart, observing our thoughts with healthy detachment, and acknowledging our feelings, saying to ourselves, for instance, "I feel anxious or fearful," "I feel confused," or "I am acting in an insecure way." We don't have to like our experience, but we do have to affirm its presence. Acceptance of our true being quiets the brain's critical voice and opens the heart to unconditional self-love.

Love of yourself can be reinforced by opening your heart at the start of each day and being mindful of your blessings and your ability to handle anything in life. It also helps to hold yourself accountable for your weaknesses, appreciate your unique gifts, and be grateful for the opportunities life has to offer.

*Opening the Heart to Link to Our True Being*

Opening the heart links us to our true being. The heart center can be highly vulnerable because it is used for channeling pure light energy while also processing emotion. Like the shutter of a camera, the heart center opens and closes and can become blocked, causing physical and emotional problems. For example, taking things "to heart" stresses this energy center, potentially resulting in physical and emotional distress—what we call a broken heart or depression. This may feel as if there is a tremendous weight pushing down on the chest, making it difficult to breathe while simultaneously causing emotional vulnerability. At such times, it is crucial to release whatever is burdening us so that our hearts can remain fully open.

When struck by light energy, the heart center creates an energetic vibration that expands and illuminates the surrounding space. As the heart center opens, we initiate an energetic pulse that receives and transmits divinely sourced information so that through our heart centers we become conduits of light force energy. Just as the heart pumps and circulates blood through the body, the heart center, or chakra—a Sanskrit word used by Hindus that means wheel of light energy—transmits light force energy through the body. In addition, the heart center is the portal for inspired information to flow from our source. Opening our hearts increases the intensity of light energy flowing through us, allowing us to receive and transmit energy that is divinely sourced. When we experience light energy flowing through our open hearts, we feel relaxed and compassionate toward everyone and everything around us, experience a sense of well-being, and have the ability to tap into energy from our source to be creative in our lives. D. H. Lawrence describes this openhearted state as "life rushing into us,"[3] while I like to describe it as light energy rushing into us.

For many of us, hearing a favorite song, experiencing a child's embrace or the image of a loved one, walking in the woods, listening to the birds, or observing the beauty of the sun setting over the horizon opens our hearts and makes us feel connected to all things. For example, if you turn the radio on in your car and hear a song that overrides your mental circuits, transporting you to another place and time, the experience is likely to open your heart, and the light energy in the form of unconditional love may fill you to a point at which you cannot contain it and want to share it with others. When my heart is open, I feel like a rose opening, with waves of warm energy vibrating within the center of my chest then emanating outward from my body in all directions. With this energetic expansion comes a sense of love, peace, and spiritual attunement with everyone and everything.

The Indian gesture of *namasté*, made by bringing together both palms of the hands before the heart and lightly bowing the head, illustrates the concept of opening the heart and the intent of accessing positive, spiritual energy through this center. Meaning "the God in me greets the God in you," the Hindu gesture pays tribute to the sacredness of all people. Perceiving ourselves and all of our relationships in this light increases our capacity to create love, joy, peace, compassion, generosity, and harmony in life.

The open heart becomes a channel for spiritual information that we can use in our daily lives. As Helen Keller said, "The best and most beautiful things in the world cannot be seen or even touched. They must be felt with the heart."[4] With an open heart, we can intuit information, bypassing the incessant chatter of our brain, and see new possibilities from an expanded perspective, enabling us to make more inspired choices.

A good example of how we can receive such information through the heart is the following experience of a client named Laura. During her daughter Anne's choral concert at school, Laura felt an excitement that something amazing was about to happen as her daughter was performing a vocal solo for the first time. As Anne began to sing, Laura felt overcome with joy and unconditional love, unable to find words to express her experience of everything melting into a stream of loving energy.

After the performance, as Laura waited in a classroom for her daughter, she was aware of a tingly electrical current of energy coursing through her body. With her heart open, she then sensed an expansion of herself, as if she were simultaneously transporting in and out of her body and to other realities. While in this state of heightened awareness, she felt clarity about a choice she had put off concerning her career. Then, like a universal translator, she sensed information being downloaded and encoded through her that would guide her to see new possibilities for her future career. Prior to this she had sensed that she needed to close her online clothing business because she wasn't making a profit, but she had been afraid of the uncertainty this situation would entail. In that instant, she looked down at the desk she was touching and wondered about a career in teaching. I later highlighted for Laura that the surge of energy had opened her to more expanded levels of spiritual awareness in which she could access information to guide her life.

When an experience opens our hearts, we all gain access to inspired information. To interpret this spiritual information we can ask ourselves, "What is the significance of my experience?" or "What am I being guided to see?" If the answer is not immediately revealed, we can let the question resound in our hearts until the answer floats through our conscious awareness, often when we least expect it, such as while awakening from sleep, showering, or driving the car. This extraordinary flow of spiritual information can also be achieved when we are engaged in an activity—such as listening to music, writing, running, or making love—in which nothing else seems to matter.

When we are intensely impacted by someone or something that enters our energy field, the shock can cause us to instinctively protect ourselves by shutting our hearts. This causes us to withdraw, feeling a sense of futility about the situation, when instead, keeping the heart open would have allowed us important access to the guidance of spirit, which can assist us in moving past whatever may be blocking our full self-expression.

## Tuning In to the Guidance of Spirit
Tuning in to the guidance of spirit helps us develop a more conscious and integrated relationship with our true being, the expression of our soul's journey through human experience. When we open our hearts and access our

true being, we invite spirit to guide us, at which point its whisper provides a flow of information we can use to make better choices in our lives.

This interaction between spirit and soul originates in age-old distinctions between the two phenomena. In the fifth century BC, Socrates and Plato supported the premise that there is an individual human spirit and a collective soul, and when the spirit leaves the body it continues on to the environment of the soul. In other words, the soul is an energetic environment like the air we breathe, a pure consciousness that everyone has the ability to access. The soul has nothing to do with our physical existence other than providing light energy that illuminates the spirit. When the spirit is lighted, the body tunes to this pure vibration. Through the divine energy connection of spirit to soul, spirit then guides us while giving us freedom to choose our life's path, and soul provides us with a blank screen on which we imprint our choices at every moment.

Realizing the choices we have in our lives and the divine right we have to make them is empowering. Similar to violinist Isaac Stern's claim that music is created in the space between the notes,[5] our spirit enlivens an otherwise insipid physical existence, providing the capacity for love, joy, and compassion in between the events of daily life and inspiring us to fully express ourselves. Music, like love, is a universal language connecting us heart and soul. Full self-expression resulting from listening to the guidance of spirit reflects our divine potential.

When we tune in to the guidance of spirit, we soon realize that this leads to a richer, more expansive way to live—even when it takes us down a more challenging path. In trusting the wisdom of spirit's guidance, we are assisted with daily problems and waste less valuable time and energy being anxious about life's difficulties. In addition, the guidance of spirit allows us to respond using expanded conscious awareness rather than react to events and relationships, giving us even greater peace of mind.

In contrast, being disconnected from the guidance of spirit diminishes our conscious awareness and traps us in the details of daily life, leaving us at the mercy of circumstances, wandering aimlessly without a sense of direction or purpose. Displaced from the high-energy spirit-to-soul link-up, we also miss the spiritual guideposts directing us and feel depressed.

For example, Craig had not tuned in to the guidance of spirit since childhood and thus had absorbed a good deal of negative programming which constantly reminded him that he was inadequate. This mindset had made him feel powerless and at the mercy of his life circumstances, unable to envision dreams beyond the details of his daily life. Fortunately, he was working on trusting himself and connecting to source when my business card, together with a gift certificate he had been given for a session, fell to the floor as he was looking through a desk drawer. Recognizing this as a spiritual sign, he overrode his abusive self-talk enough to call me.

To avoid being disconnected from the guidance of spirit, it is necessary to acknowledge yourself as a strong and sensitive person connected to source and open to new information coming through your heart. This perspective will help you view life experiences of all sorts as opportunities to fulfill your soul potential.

The following story about my client Sharon is a good example of opening the heart and tuning in to the guidance of spirit to gain information that inspires more fulfilling choices in life. At age ten, Sharon had been diagnosed with chronic fatigue syndrome, which had significantly limited her participation in activities because she was exhausted most of the time. Consequently, she felt as if her illness had become a way of life. By the time she started working with me at age fifteen, Sharon had spent most of her life suffering from physical pain and depression. Being a highly sensitive person, she often absorbed other people's negative energies and internalized their suffering. Deferring mostly to the needs of others, she had not explored her own creative energies, developed her personal power, or made choices that expressed her core being.

After working with me for several years, Sharon began to see that she was caught between two realities—one projected by the beliefs and patterns surrounding her illness and the other depicting the world of full self-expression that she was afraid to enter. Through expanding her conscious awareness she saw she needed to take responsibility for her health, attitudes, and thoughts and be completely free of negative patterns running her life so she could choose how to use her energy positively at any given moment. In addition, she had to develop the stamina and courage to break free of those people and situations that had not only contributed to her illness but also didn't support her well-being and spiritual growth.

In the safe space of unconditional love with me and her support team, she learned to release negative patterns that prevented her from trusting herself and opening her heart. As she experienced loving acceptance, her wounds and fears surfaced to be healed, and she was able to see herself as a strong, competent, and lovable young woman. Eventually aligning more with her true being, Sharon realized it was time to follow her heart's desires. After graduating from high school with her GED, she dedicated the following summer to discovering her desires and opening to new experiences. She soon began tuning in to the guidance of spirit and gained information that encouraged her to channel her energies into ballroom dancing, volunteering for an animal shelter, and discovering new people and places. She permitted herself to fully participate in a myriad of experiences and gained guidance from spirit that would ultimately influence her future choices.

Once we begin receiving such spiritual information, we can use both hindsight and insight to gain foresight, the ability to envision future results of our thoughts, feelings, and choices. Foresight allows us to bypass moments, months, or even years of life's lessons. Through this window of expanded conscious awareness we can see, for example, that it may no longer be valuable to trudge through the pain and drama of certain circumstances or relationships. Consequently, we become more proactive and present and future oriented.

It has been said that "what lies behind us and what lies before us are tiny matters compared to what lies within us."[6] And indeed, the guidance of spirit will constantly remind you of who you are and what your heart most desires even when you choose to ignore the information. The more you open your heart and gain access to this guidance, the more you expand your perspective, which will allow you to consciously override the mental noise that may threaten to overwhelm your true being. Then instead of adhering to the ego-induced dictates of your analytical brain you can instead follow your heart's desires. When we are guided by spirit, we experience our mistakes as divine opportunities to transform our lives.

### Listening to the Voice of Spirit Speaking through the Heart

Over the years, many people have asked me how I distinguish between information coming from my head and information coming from my heart, as well as how I use my head but follow my heart. Learning to differentiate the fear-based patterns of the brain from the voice of spirit speaking through the heart requires expanding conscious awareness through becoming a conscious observer of our experience and engaging in disciplined practice.

The point of view we see with our heads is that of the analytical brain, which views life from a limited perspective and only one aspect of conscious awareness—the past. The brain is like a computer that can scan, access, and store data mechanically, but because it does not tap into creational energy it can only use the information that we provide it. This information often takes the form of negative mindsets, beliefs, and patterns stored on its "hard drive." For example, it employs such fear-based dictates as "Be careful not to let your guard down," "If you take that risk you'll get hurt," and "Don't confide in anybody, because they'll let you down," all of which eventually produce a lack of trust in our own experience and restrict the quality of the choices we make. Accessing such negative files, the brain can only report on the data they contain.

In addition, because of its hard wiring, when the brain moves into survival mode it shuts down to protect itself from any new experience it does not recognize as a past mental file, including new information coming from the voice of spirit. Past mental files stored in the brain program us to think that only logical thought is valid. Operating from such a basis distorts information coming through our conscious awareness, which creates conflict between our heads and our hearts. This short-circuits the flow of spiritual information, producing an energy block. The brain is then given permission to accept what has been stored and is reinforced as the master of our reality. In contrast, the voice of spirit speaking through our heart provides information from an expanded point of view, validates present-oriented experiences, and guides us without judgment. It whispers, "I know" instead of "I think," "I trust" instead of "I believe," and "I create" instead of "I wait."

Listening to the voice of spirit speaking through the heart requires making an effort to nurture a more introspective and integrated relationship with ourselves. It is often difficult to find time in our busy lives to be quiet and listen inwardly. Our minds are filled with endless to-do lists, obligations, and distractions. We are constantly making excuses for not having the time to develop an intimate, loving relationship with ourselves. Unfortunately, these circumstances set us up to follow the dictates of the ego instead of our true being. Many people have revealed to me how difficult it is to stop the incessant ricochet of thoughts that prompts their constant anxiety. Unfortunately, we spend most of our time playing out past events or worrying about future outcomes, which interrupts our experience of the present moment. More often than not, we hear the voice in our heads that judges us instead of the loving, guiding voice of spirit through our hearts. Solitude and introspection, however, helps us open our hearts, gain knowledge and appreciation of our true being, and, guided by spirit, begin to make choices without relying on others for validation. In these reflective states we experience our connection to source as a channel of light energy.

Because of the importance of opening our hearts and listening to the voice of spirit, it is advantageous to set aside time each day for quiet reflection and meditation, whether walking in a labyrinth, sitting in a garden or on a park bench, soaking in a bathtub, or journaling, trying each day to increase the length of time spent alone without diversions. It does not matter where, when, or how we spend this time. What matters is that the sacred space we create is a safe sanctuary and that we view the act as a covenant with ourselves to assure future happiness, which we can achieve by tuning to the vibration of the heart.

Observing ourselves without judgment or resistance, we can watch how our incessant mental dictates surface, then simply allow them to move through the mind. We can further cue our brains to step aside by touching the center of the chest, using a mantra like "Open heart," or consciously directing our attention to the heart. Such simple cues help us let go of our negative thoughts and focus on our connection with source through our open heart.

Sustained time alone also assists us in distinguishing our negative fear-based thought processes from positive spiritual information channeled through our heart. Journaling during these times can help us bypass the brain-induced ego and fear-based thoughts to make us aware of the voice of spirit speaking through our hearts.

While quiet and solitude promote a meditative state, we can also experience such a state by approaching daily activities like cooking, cleaning, washing dishes, eating, shopping, walking, and driving with mindfulness, participating in them with the intention of being fully present and enjoying the moment. For example, while walking we can focus on the larger significance of our movements by observing how stepping forward signifies advancing toward the future, releasing a back foot means letting go of the past, and the space between our steps represents being in the present. Learning to quiet the mind, open the heart, and allow the whole body, including the brain, to align with this energy coming through the heart promotes a state of internal congruence in which we can listen to the voice of spirit and receive guidance for our choices.

Another way I teach clients to do this is by asking them to sit in a chair and touch the center of their chest, which immediately cues them to direct their attention from their heads to their hearts. As they attend to their heart center, I ask them to focus on the ebb and flow of their breathing. Using their breath as a focal point, I suggest that they breathe in love and breathe out fear. Then I encourage them to practice opening their hearts while observing the incessant thoughts that move through their minds, such as the unfinished grocery list, the discussion they want to have with their boss, or the phone call they forgot to return. When distracted by such thoughts, they can again touch the center of their chests to focus their attention back to their hearts, surrender to self-awareness, and listen to the voice of spirit giving them new possibilities for choices in their lives. In this way, instead of mind over matter, they can achieve heart over mind and gain valuable guidance from spirit.

### Becoming Our Own Loving Coach

To respond to life circumstances proactively rather than reactively, we need to see ourselves in a positive light by reminding ourselves that we are doing the best we can, forgiving ourselves for our past erroneous choices, and visualizing ourselves moving forward and making better choices in the future. In becoming our own loving coach and trusting the voice of spirit through our hearts, we learn how to eliminate self-abusive thoughts, beliefs, and words and replace them with positive ones. By coaching ourselves to override the brain's negative programming, we begin to distinguish between the patterns that have run our lives in the past and new possibilities currently suggested by the voice of spirit speaking through the heart. While listening to this voice, we identify and disrupt the negative encoding that tells us we are inadequate or have made bad decisions in the past. When we become aware of such negative messages, we can listen without condemnation and talk to ourselves as a loving coach, then guide ourselves to release the negative mentality that triggers these patterns and support positive intentions.

One tool we can use to clear negative mental patterns is positive affirmations. For this purpose it may at first be necessary to use positive affirmations many times a day. But with practice, we can train ourselves to override these fear-based thoughts with a simple positive phrase to remind ourselves to disengage from them. Here are a few positive affirmations you can say aloud when you witness a negative thought, mindset, or belief cropping up: "Move beyond," "Open and let go," and "Bless and release." Using these phrases repeatedly over time will disrupt the automatic reaction of negative thinking. And whenever you feel afraid to face circumstances, you can override your anxiety by using such phrases as "Take a step," "Move forward," or "Make a choice." These verbal phrases will help ease you out of your comfort zone, make new choices, and stretch yourself spiritually.

Being our own loving coach allows us to release everything that keeps us stuck in a holding pattern. These releases occur each time the icy grip of a perceived limitation is exposed to the warmth of our self-love. Eventually, we can more easily open the heart and channel light energy to project the positive aspects of our being, enabling us to create the relationship opportunities we have always wanted.

PRACTICING THE PRINCIPLES IN CHAPTER TWO

1. *Practice opening and expanding the heart center.* Touching the center of your chest, experience the ebb and flow of your breathing. Each time you inhale take in life force energy as oxygen, and each time you exhale release negative thoughts, emotions, and physical discomfort. The deeper you breathe, the more you get in touch with the core of your being. Now quiet your mind and witness your thoughts, focusing on the flow of energy emanating from your heart so you can view a greater range of possibilities and see what your heart desires.

2. *Begin every day by affirming the value of your experiences and feeling grateful for opportunities to open your heart.* No matter what your circumstances, daily bless yourself, your fellow human beings, and the earth; then express appreciation for your unique gifts. An affirmation that can be helpful in this regard is the following by poet e. e. cummings reminding us to affirm ourselves and life in this way: "I thank you God for this most amazing day: for the leaping greenly spirits of trees and a blue true dream of sky: and for everything which is natural which is infinite which is yes."[7] This opens your heart and sets your intention to hear the voice of spirit for guidance in life.

3. *Practice listening to the voice of spirit through your heart.* Create your own safe sanctuary for exploring yourself, such as sitting in a park, garden, or on a front porch; walking in nature; soaking in a pool or bath; or meditating in a favorite room or chair. Take time every day for being still or meditating, gradually increasing the length of time you remain alone and quiet, without distractions, to listen to the voice of spirit through your heart.

4. *Incorporate journaling into your life to open your heart and listen to the voice of spirit.* Journaling can assist you in observing your circumstances and thus help you release negative mindsets and open your heart to inner truth. Record any

negative thoughts, feelings, or behaviors and what they suggest. Whenever you observe yourself using negative self-talk, write down positive affirmations that override your brain's programming. Review your journal entries to observe any patterns of negative thoughts, feelings, or behaviors so you can recognize them when they arise in the future.

5. *Become your own loving coach.* Override your negative mental patterns by eliminating self-abusive words and actions, such as "I am inadequate" or "I'll never be happy." Disrupt the chain reaction of your negative thinking with positive affirmations such as "See and move beyond," "Open and let go," or "Bless and release," saying these mantras aloud or to yourself so they can become the basis for manifesting the fulfilling life you envision.

6. *Practice loving-kindness, nonjudgment, and acceptance of yourself and others.* As you move through your day, keep an open heart and extend unconditional love to whomever you meet. In these moments, reflect on the connection between your heart and the other person's. Then bless the individual. This tool can be used to release blame or judgment and to more quickly forgive yourself or others.

# Chapter Three
## RECOGNIZING PATTERNS

"We shall not cease from exploration,
and the end of all our exploring will be to arrive
where we started and know the place for the first time."

—T. S. ELLIOT

*T*HE JOURNEY TOWARD SOUL-HEARTED PARTNERSHIP compels us to clear away everything that impedes our ability to express our fullest potential. Entering into such a partnership with ourselves and then another motivates us to become aware of how every thought, feeling, and choice either supports or interferes with this expression. Then upon expanding our conscious awareness, we gain the spiritual perspective necessary to recognize our behavioral patterns and how they can block the flow of energy required for personal transformation and healthy relationships.

To free ourselves from the influence of such patterns, we must first awaken from the spellbound sleep induced by these entrancing patterns, and recognize how they operate in our lives. As we access and use our expanded conscious awareness through our hearts, we can clearly observe and flag the behavioral patterns that undermine the expression of our core being. Having identified them, we can then release them and direct the flow of our creative energies to manifest a more fulfilling life.

## Positive and Negative Patterns

Human beings are creatures of habit who, when conditioned, tend to behave automatically in certain circumstances. For example, when we see a police officer waving traffic through a stop sign, we may still stop out of habit, or we may set an alarm clock even though we are not working the next day. We can also easily adopt patterns that, when repeated habitually, coalesce into an identity structure that undermines the expression of our core being and dictates our lives in ways not conducive to fully realizing our dreams. In her book *Anatomy of the Spirit*, Caroline Myss supports this premise when she says, "Habit is a hell to which people cling in an attempt to stop the flow of change."[1] Breaking the repetition of patterns, on the other hand, allows us to channel our creative energy and supports personal transformation.

Patterns in themselves are not negative. For example, in the natural world patterns and cycles perpetuate life, such as the changing seasons, the rings of trees, the spirals of shells, or the orbits of planets, which exist because of nature's forces and reflect healthy growth or transformation. Having a conscious awareness of participating in the cyclical transformations of life affords us a spiritual clarity that promotes healing and a sense of wholeness. The naturalist Rachel Carson describes the value of such awareness of transitions in *The Sense of Wonder*: "Those who contemplate the beauty of the earth find reserves of strength that will endure as long as life lasts. . . . There is something infinitely healing in the repeated refrains of nature—the assurance that dawn comes after night, and spring after winter."[2]

Human patterns used as defense mechanisms, including overreactions to circumstances, however, become detrimental, leading to physical, mental, or emotional self-destructive behavior, and as such, must be uprooted. By analogy, under negative conditions a maple sapling can become overwhelmed by parasitic vines that feed off of its life force. Pruning the vines only stops their growth temporarily; stopping it altogether requires pulling the vines out by their roots. Like these parasitic vines, negative patterns block the flow of energy needed for healthy growth. To alter the course of our lives enough to enter into a soul-hearted relationship with ourselves and others, we have to use our conscious awareness to recognize and release the negative patterns.

Examples of patterns that interrupt the flow of positive energy are seeking approval; avoidance; defiance; need to control; obligation; fear; judging things as good/bad, right/wrong; impatience; rejection; resistance; resentment; revenge; righteous indignation; self-preservation; being self-sacrificial or passive-aggressive; and all-or-nothing thinking in terms of success/failure and winning/losing. For many of us, such behavioral patterns typify daily life. And left unchecked, they drain life force energy necessary for making more discerning choices in general and in our relationships.

Let's take a closer look at some of the most destructive patterns in human relationships—those of right/wrong, good/bad, and win/lose. The unfortunate consequences of such toxic patterns are judgment, blame, and punishment, which undermine all kinds of relationships and make it difficult for people to accept each other's differences. When individuals focus on these polarities rather on their spiritual connections with one another, they perpetuate feelings of resentment and rejection, which cause them to feel trapped.

The patterns of right/wrong, good/bad, and win/lose are insidious in relationships. The refusal to honor another person's right to a point of view and instead devaluing the individual instigates a power struggle. Making the individual feel wrong, bad, or like a loser may offer a temporary feeling of vindication and control, but getting stuck in these polarities can prevent the harmonious resolution of problems, the flow of positive energy, and the embracing of new possibilities.

For instance, suppose you and your partner have a joint checking account and you find out that a check your partner wrote has bounced. You immediately blame your partner for the overdraft rather than first finding out what actually happened. Later, you notice that you forgot to record several checks and to balance the checkbook. In such a situation, to restore harmony in the relationship acknowledge the mistake and let go of the whole notion of right versus wrong. In all relationships, the pattern of right/wrong serves no purpose, closes off vital life force energy, and perpetuates toxicity instead of well-being.

Another pattern that erodes our sense of well-being and affects our relationships is resentment. Harboring resentments about how other people have treated us is a self-destructive pattern that leads to feeling rejected. In holding on to resentment we end up rejecting ourselves. At such times, anger, hurt, righteous indignation, and a desire for revenge permeates our interactions with ourselves and others, which constricts the flow of positive energy through the heart.

This insidious pattern has its origin in feeling unloved and worthless. When we seek love based on external sources or circumstances, we set up an expectation that love and acceptance come from outside of us. In reaction, we become highly sensitive to what people say, feel, and do, setting ourselves up for being ejected from situations. For example, suppose you call a friend and leave a message that you are going to be in the area and would like to drop off a package at her home. Instead of just depositing the package on the doorstep, you secretly expect to spend time together. But when you arrive you realize she is not home, at which point your pattern of rejection quickly surfaces and you become angry and hurt. Feeding your rejection pattern, you make the assumption that she did not want to spend time with you. Then instead of talking to your friend, getting more information, and clearing your negativity, you react with disappointment and leave a nasty message on her voice mail. Later, you find out she was shopping for groceries and other items and never received your first message. By this time, you have already made your friend wrong and ejected yourself from the relationship.

An additional behavioral pattern that adversely affects most people's lives is obligation. Mental dictates such as "I must" or "I should" can get us into situations in which we would rather not be involved, such as going to a family social gathering we would prefer not to attend. The pattern of obligation can also be triggered when a person suddenly calls and asks if you are free without telling you the plans they have in mind. You then may feel obligated to answer "yes," leaving you vulnerable to committing to an event in which you may have no interest. In such situations, it is essential that you pause and, without judgment, observe the source of your pattern that threatens your sense of well-being. Next, respond from a more positive perspective—for instance, asking if you can call the person back. Finally, affirm to yourself that you always have the power of choice and inform the person of your preference.

Another pattern harmful to relationships is the need to control. Many of us experience a need to control everything as we repeatedly avoid recognizing and releasing emotional pain, which is often disguised as fear and anxiety. Whenever we micromanage someone or something, we are likely feeling insecure and out of control ourselves. In fact, we develop the pattern to infuse our lives with a sense of internal security and predictability, especially when we are beset by survival issues, such as earning a living, finding a partner, and taking care of physical needs. Unfortunately, this fear-based pattern actually generates an illusion of stability, displacing an absolute trust in ourselves and our connection with source onto external conditions such as who we are with, what we do, where we live, or what we own. As a result, we come to believe we are victims of circumstance, lacking the power to manifest the lives we want. When using control as a coping mechanism, we eventually find it easier to hide within this self-destructive comfort zone and avoid facing what stands in the way of living a healthy and happy life.

The pattern of need for control also is prevalent in relationships, for example, when one person, as caretaker, reinforces the other person's victim pattern. Within such a relationship dynamic, one person needs to dominate the other to feel secure and more powerful. Unfortunately, this also fosters helplessness and stifles full self-expression of the other. We see this demonstrated when one person tells the other what to think, feel, or choose, and the other person becomes dependent on them for making *any* choices, eventually deferring to others without knowing they themselves are operating out of fear. Automatically yielding to the desires of others only compromises our own heart's desires and reinforces the fear-based pattern of seeking approval. Most importantly, when we focus on whatever it takes to please others, even if it means diminishing what we cherish, we deplete our energies for manifesting new positive choices in life.

To identify the patterns in which we habitually engage, it is necessary to take note of which people and circumstances push our buttons and trigger our negative reactions. The stronger these reactions are, the more deeply ingrained the patterns and the more important it is to discover and face their origins in order to eventually release them.

As we become more aware of our patterns, we can choose to spend less or no time with certain people and in particular situations to avoid triggering negative reactions. To minimize relationship choices based on such patterns, it is important to open the heart and listen to the voice of spirit guiding us to stay true to ourselves while at the same time noticing and releasing our conditioned patterns.

## Sources of Patterns

Our patterns originate from the negative messages we absorb beginning in early childhood. We observe these behavioral patterns in role models such as parents, caregivers, and even well-meaning mentors and friends, often developing them as coping mechanisms for meeting life's challenges and disappointments. Like Snow White, enticed by the wicked witch to take a bite from the poisoned apple, we tend to gradually succumb to the deadening spell of these lethal messages. Then, at each successive stage of life we are influenced by the negative messages and behaviors of new role models and relationship experiences.

Our first subtle impressions of relationship patterns begin at birth, with our caregivers as our first role models. As children, we are dependent on them for love and care, which makes us highly susceptible to negative patterns they may exhibit. Depending on a caregiver as the source of unconditional love sets up the illusion that the source of our happiness and well-being comes from outside of us. As a result, many individuals spend their entire lives seeking approval—affirmation from others that they are lovable—instead of seeing themselves as a source of unconditional love.

As children, we implicitly follow the voice of spirit through our hearts. The subsequent acceptance of our experience, including thoughts, feelings, and sensations, is the essence of our true being. But then, when these experiences are questioned or invalidated by negative mindsets, beliefs, and patterns of caregivers, we begin to doubt ourselves, which compromises our ability to trust our conscious awareness and take responsibility for what we think, feel, and do.

Later, tuning out the voice of spirit speaking through the heart, we allow negative patterns to ultimately silence our true being, form a structured identity, and behave habitually. The hard shell of an identity resulting from such programming resides solely in the brain. As we become more invested in this identity, we begin to believe that it defines us, and we operate from this persona rather than from our true being. Living our lives and relating to others through such patterns produces conflict when we begin to tune in to any new information from the voice of spirit as it guides us through the heart.

The following story about my client Elise illustrates how invalidation of trust in experience can contribute to the development of such patterns as abandonment, need for approval, and sense of futility. At age eight, growing up in Ireland, Elise felt an intimate connection with her mother that went beyond the sharing of the same first name. Standing next to her mother as they watched fireworks from their front porch one evening, a strong sense of her mother's impending death swept over her like a cold breath. Six months later, Elise awoke with an intuition that her mother's death was imminent and pleaded with her mother to let her stay home from school that day. Ignoring her desperate cries, her mother took Elise by the hand and dragged her kicking and screaming to school. Early the next morning, while Elise lay sleeping beside her mother, the woman quietly died.

Following her mother's death, Elise wanted to grieve her loss but this opportunity was denied her. On the day of her mother's wake, she was given an ice cream cone and sent outside to play while the adult family members sat inside supporting one another in their grief. As she sat in her mother's favorite rocking chair eating her ice cream cone, unbeknownst to her, as her ice cream quickly melted away, so did her girlhood innocence and expression of her true being.

Such actions by her caregivers taught Elise that she couldn't act on her own experience following the voice of spirit guiding her through her heart. Thus she learned early on to tune out this guidance and defer to others, dismissing her connection to her true being as a survival mechanism.

In *The Drama of the Gifted Child*, Alice Miller suggests that there is significant pressure on us as children to deny our true being and take on false selves to please our parents or caregivers. Thus growing up, we often face a difficult choice—to maintain our connection with our true being or be loved. If we choose to maintain our link to our true being, we risk abandonment by our parents or caregivers, and if we select conditional love we abandon our true being. Many of us choose to abandon ourselves so that we can receive love and thus handle the circumstances of life.

During adolescence, teachers, best friends, mentors, and even the dominant culture portrayed through the media become our role models for relationships. When these role models exhibit fear-based, self-destructive patterns, we frequently repress our full self-expression and adopt those patterns. Mary Pipher, in *Reviving Ophelia*, suggests that young girls' sense of being can be fragmented by the chaos of adolescence if loving, trustworthy, and competent role models are missing from their lives. This happens because of the physical, emotional, and spiritual changes that they experience without a support system to guide them on this journey of individuation. The resulting loss of wholeness, self-confidence, and self-direction can last well into adulthood.

Over time, the patterns being triggered by negative thoughts, mindsets, and belief systems are stored on the hard drive of our brain regardless of whether we are aware of them. Subsequently, as adults we perpetuate self-defensive patterns we have learned whenever a circumstance triggers them—usually situations that induce fear, sadness, disappointment, or disillusionment. This is because later in life the brain retrieves the file stored on its hard drive, often when we least expect it, and we suffer the painful consequences without even understanding our emotional reactions.

For example, we may have been warned by a parent or caregiver that we would get sick if we went outside without a coat. Later, as an adult, when we walk outside without a coat our brain finds this stored fear-based message and we feel guilty about our actions or actually become sick due to the power of the mind's suggestion. Although becoming sick has nothing to do with walking outside without a coat, it may in fact relate to the break we need from daily stresses but have not justified giving ourselves. Unless we see our behavior from the detached perspective of conscious awareness, we often have no idea of the source of information the brain has accessed and are thus unaware of the motivations behind our thoughts, feelings, and actions. With healthy detachment, however, it becomes possible to trace patterns to family history, early development, or past experience.

In tracing the origins of my own negative patterns, I have had to recognize and release those involving fear, abandonment, and the need to be a caretaker, which are deeply rooted in my early childhood experiences. As a child, these programmed patterns served a protective purpose; however, at age twenty-six I realized, as the fabric of my life began to unravel, that my survival patterns had outworn their welcome.

My negative patterns developed as a result of being physically and emotionally abandoned by my mother, which led to my taking responsibility for the care of my two brothers. When I was seven, my parents divorced and I went to live with my mother and two younger brothers in a rundown tenement apartment in a neighborhood far from my home. As my mother's drug addiction and self-destructive behavior spiraled out of control, seeing no alternative I realized that my own and my brothers' survival depended on me and thus became their surrogate mother. This meant that the little girl in me had to step aside, and instead I received on-the-job training in this pattern of caretaker. I would eventually learn how to apply its survival skills in every situation I would experience, except in caring for myself.

After my mother was taken to a psychiatric institution following a suicide attempt, then escaped with a fellow patient while on a field trip, she deserted us for good. As a result, the pattern of abandonment became ingrained in my behavior. I spent the next twenty years pretending my mother had never existed, suppressing any memories and feelings that reminded me of her, and burying my feelings of anger, hurt, and sadness deep inside me to avoid the pain of abandonment. I even ignored the voice of spirit through my heart and in this way abandoned myself. The more I saw myself as unlovable, the more this myth became a self-fulfilling prophecy and kept loving, healthy relationships from manifesting.

Following my college graduation, I married my first husband, and we moved to North Carolina so he could attend law school. Afraid to be alone, I had prevailed over an earlier instinct to break off the engagement and attend graduate school instead. So I postponed graduate school and began working as a special education teacher in a deprived, poverty-stricken school district to support us. Prior to his graduation from law school, I applied to psychology graduate programs, excited that it was finally my turn to follow my dreams. But a few weeks after I was accepted into the doctoral program at Kent State University, I found out that I was unexpectedly pregnant.

The thought of having a child unleashed a wave of unresolved grief that I could no longer suppress. I felt flung back into my past, which brought up unexpressed feelings of loss so painful that I wanted to die rather than face motherhood. I was terrified of repeating my mother's parental legacy by abandoning my child and losing myself. The catalyst for recognizing my patterns came with the birth of this first child, a son. New motherhood even encouraged me to let go of my unresolved grief, unhealthy patterns, and transform my life.

Reflecting on this time, I now know that, as in the movie *Groundhog Day*, I had been going through the motions and doing what I thought everyone else wanted me to do. I had been on the outside of my life peering in, thinking it would someday begin. Suddenly responsible for a baby, however, I emerged, as if from a coma, wanting to resolve what had been holding me back from fully living.

At this point I met the two most influential mentors of my life, my therapist Roberta and spiritual teacher Bryan, and through therapeutic and spiritual inner work, managed to trace the source of my pain and patterns back to the crucible moment I had lost my mother. In doing this, I realized that my inner spirit had never disappeared, despite the fact that I had disconnected from my true being to escape my grief, thereby diminishing my ability to see the truth of my circumstances.

With the assistance of my therapist and spiritual teacher, I began to see that my pattern of abandonment and need to be a caretaker had surfaced in every relationship I had experienced. I recognized that from the start I had yearned for a knight in shining armor, thinking he would fulfill my needs for security and nurturing. Therefore, when my high school sweetheart and best friend proposed marriage after I graduated from college, I considered him my prince. A supportive man whom I deeply respected and loved, he made my life feel safe and predictable, and I thought he would rescue me from the emptiness I sensed inside myself, making me feel complete. But because of my unfulfilled need for security and nurturing, my patterns still surfaced.

I saw that over time I had habitually sacrificed my own needs to tend to those of others, with the assumption that no one would care for me. This need for affiliation and genuine love drove me to choose men who depended on me for fulfilling their dreams. In such situations I felt valued, competent, and powerful—in other words, sufficiently distracted from my despair to be able to sometimes fool myself into thinking I had filled the void I felt inside. What I did not realize then was that everything I needed to fill the inner void was already inside me—a connection with my spiritual source.

To recognize patterns, we need to first become aware of the "flags" telling us that existing negative patterns are operating. This sort of information usually surfaces in situations involving pain or fear that engage the brain in survival dynamics; often, simply a word, glance, or the slightest interaction can cause them to erupt in a defensive reaction. One common flag informing us of an existing pattern is the obsessive attachment to a certain outcome, grievance, or position. Other flags are the urgent need to defend ourselves, be right, or blame someone.

In identifying such flags we have an opportunity to eliminate the underlying patterns at their source, together with the physical and emotional reactions that have evolved from them. To trace their origins, it is useful to journal, speak with friends, or talk to a therapist. To discover more about the source of our patterns, we can reflect on why we keep putting ourselves in certain negative situations with particular people and if the taproot of these patterns is perhaps the need for security, stability, or status. Arriving at the ultimate source of our negative patterns gives us a chance to release them so we can see our inherent wholeness and the fact that at our core we are radiant divine beings.

### The Cyclical Nature of Patterns

Patterns will recur continuously until their source is recognized and released. Like clams, patterns dig deep for defense and regenerate, producing the same results repeatedly until they are identified and released. When we ignore them or attempt to run away from them, we cannot help but fall into their grip over and over again. Accessing our conscious awareness and allowing ourselves to be guided by spirit, however, empowers us to eliminate these self-destructive patterns and make healthier choices in life.

Making the decision to identify and break the cyclical nature of a negative pattern is like facing a fork in the road. One trajectory, presided over by spirit, leads us through the healing process in which we recognize and release the pattern and attain well-being. The other trajectory, governed by the brain, leads us to simply replace the existing pattern with a subtler version of it so we remain in our comfort zone of unhealthiness without having to actually transform ourselves. For instance, we may substitute aggressive behavior such as yelling with passive prolonged silence after the end of a relationship, leading invariably to another unhealthy relationship, in which we repeat a different pattern of emotional manipulation. To recognize and release negative patterns, we must choose the path presided over by spirit, which gives us liberating information beyond our fear-based thoughts. With spirit's guidance we become empowered to replace negative patterns with positive behaviors, resulting in a healthier lifestyle.

Spirit always guides us in healthy directions. For example, it can influence us to establish new affirmations, like "I can stop smoking," "I can metabolize weight," "I can create the work I love," "I can have healthy relationships," and "I can do these things with gentleness, assuredness, and ease." Or it can guide us to go for a walk instead of going to lunch when we are not hungry, to spend time with people who love us unconditionally, and to take time out to release stress and care for our bodies. Spirit can also guide us to walk out of situations or relationships that are unhealthy for us. It can even send valuable messages through the people we consider "earth angels" and respond to our prayers to produce better outcomes in challenging situations.

An example of the cyclical nature of a pattern when it is left unrecognized and unreleased is the following. My client Robert felt as if he had been running away from himself all his life. Tired of feeling needy and running into the arms of anyone who would take care of him, he attempted to disconnect from his painful past, going so far as to change his name and relocate from his hometown. But even then, not knowing who he really was and feeling like a phony he perpetuated the patterns of avoidance, dependency, and playing victim.

Then Robert met Paula and felt an instant soul connection, the kind of electricity that occurs between two people who seem to have known each other for their entire lives. This was the first experience of real relationship he had ever felt. At the same time, however, he was terrified of becoming involved in an exclusive, intimate relationship.

First, I assisted Robert in realizing that the more he avoided facing himself and the choices he had made in his life the worse his patterns would be, if only to get his attention. He had put himself in a box constructed of his own patterned identity. It was time for him to see himself and his life from a fresh perspective, and this new relationship was giving him a chance to recognize unhealthy patterns and release them. But he knew that if he chose to fully enter into the relationship he would have to confront his unresolved painful past and uncover his patterns.

Eventually opening his heart and using his expanded awareness, Robert recognized that running away from himself was no longer an option. He acknowledged that to develop the kind of relationship he truly desired he had to break the cyclical, self-destructive patterns of avoidance, dependency, and playing victim by uprooting them at their source. Seeing the opportunity for a loving, healthy relationship gave Robert the courage to face the pain that had had him running in the first place.

Robert's situation underscores how easy it is to continue ignoring self-destructive patterns and causing ourselves further suffering. Like Robert, we too can feel compelled at last to recognize and eliminate them. This becomes possible by identifying the cyclical patterns in every situation then trusting the guidance of spirit to move us beyond them and provide more positive alternatives.

## Relationships Built on Patterns

Tragically, relationships are often built on patterns instead of on the combined energies of two fully expressed individuals. This becomes most apparent when one or both individuals need external validation of their own existence. Having moved initially from the support of family, early friends, and school mentors to the relationship with their spouse or partner, they seek affirmation of their identity from additional external sources, instead of from the core of their being. They feel good if they are wealthy, hold a position of authority, have social status, a significant other who is successful, and bright children. If, on the other hand, their close relationship deteriorates, they may immediately try to get involved in another relationship to once again feel loved and validated. In the frenzy of moving from one relationship to the next, they fail to develop a fully expressed relationship with themselves—which is the basis of any healthy relationship with another.

The underlying problem is that such individuals remain under the spell of their patterns. Thus when they initiate relationships without listening to the voice of spirit guiding them, their relationships are built on nothing more than a matching of the patterns of two individuals. Indeed, we tend to be attracted to individuals with patterns that fit well with our own. But because these relationships break down when we repeat our negative patterns, they fail to generate a positive flow of energy. Try as we might to make such relationships work, they cannot unless we take the necessary steps to transform ourselves.

As a psychotherapist I have witnessed many relationships plagued by behavioral problems, especially among people with bipolar or passive-aggressive patterns. Often the afflicted person behaves in such a manner that the partner not only reinforces these dysfunctional patterns but also reacts in a similar fashion, feeding off of the negative energy. The emotional cycles in this kind of relationship resemble the highs and lows of mania and depression, with each person sharing the responsibility for perpetuating such patterns. This happens because we take on the behaviors we resist if we do not recognize and eliminate them.

When we stay in relationships that support such patterns, we compromise both ourselves and our partner. In thinking we have little power to let go of our unhealthy relationships, we settle for their deadening effects rather than healing those aspects of ourselves that interfere with our ability to cultivate soul-hearted partnerships.

Often, however, we choose relationships subconsciously as occasions to recognize and release negative patterns. These patterns tend to surface more frequently as a relationship becomes increasingly exclusive and we begin to feel safe in it. Feeling safe in a relationship then offers the opportunity to explore the unwanted patterns. Being in an intimate relationship with someone who enables us to recognize our patterns can give us the courage to eliminate them and also give our partner the chance to recognize and eliminate their own. Of course, a partner unprepared to interact at this higher level of spiritual awareness may simply leave and either find someone else or remain alone, convinced they will never find a significant other.

Relationships built on the facade of enmeshed patterns inhibit full self-expression, whereas soul-hearted partnerships support the release of patterns and the full expression of each person's core being. As the individuals reach a level of spiritual development that helps them see they can actively choose their destiny, they realize it is not necessary to repeat the destructive patterns of the past. To truly alter the course of their reality, they have to then become proactive in eliminating the patterns. Acknowledging that patterns are part of the human condition allows us to accept them without judgment and then to release them.


## Coaddictive Patterns in Relationships

Coaddictive patterns often lead us to participate in a parade of superficial relationships, emotional crutches we lean on to avoid facing our fears and insecurities. Looking for security outside of ourselves ultimately keeps us distracted from our feelings of spiritual disconnection. And relationships woven of the coaddictive patterns of two people keeps them both distracted from developing a fully realized relationship with themselves.

Addictions are fixes that mask our deep-seated issues so that we can avoid dealing with them constructively. We may even create addictions to the patterns of struggle and suffering, which feed on negativity, diminish our ability to sustain healthy relationships, and in the extreme form, contribute to an identity structure such as caretaker, victim, or survivor.

Self-destructive patterns of addiction occur when we abandon personal responsibility and expect others to create our lives for us. Displacing our needs and desires onto someone else, we substitute a physical dependence for a spiritual connection. Feeling disconnected from ourselves and our source, we float through life waiting for a fairy tale to define our purpose, assuming it will show up in the form of "the right relationship." We project this fantasy, shifting the burden of responsibility for manifesting the real-life version onto someone else. Expecting someone to fulfill our dreams, we dismiss the power we have to create them for ourselves and then wonder why we feel perpetually disappointed with life. But eventually we discover that no relationship ever rescues us; we have to rescue ourselves.

Relationships in which neither person takes full responsibility for expressing and satisfying their own needs result in no one's needs ever being fully satisfied. Instead of asking for or manifesting what they want, partners become masterful at tolerating mediocrity. Then, due to their patterns of needing to fix the other person or be fixed, the individuals drain the life force out of the relationship.

A common type of coaddictive relationship is one based on the roles of caretaker and victim. Such relationships develop out of one person's desire to be taken care of (victim) and the other's wish to be needed (caretaker). In many of these relationships, the caretakers started out as caregivers. A true caregiver opens her heart compassionately in healthy detachment and maintains a positive flow of energy with her partner without suffering with him. But in coaddictive relationships victims often attract someone who will take care of them without giving much in return. When this happens, the caregiver takes responsibility for the victim's life, becoming a caretaker and enabling the victim to continue a dependency on them to fulfill personal needs. In such circumstances caretakers can become resentful and controlling when there is no balanced contribution or exchange of energy within the relationship.

The pattern of victim, on the other hand, coalesces into a chronic dependency in which the person feels he must obtain the energy he needs from another power source. Many people have had the experience of feeling drained just being in the presence of such energy vampires. In this way, victims surrender control of their lives, forfeiting not only their ability as a power source but also their access to conscious awareness and the courage to shift their lives.

Let's take a look at a coaddictive relationship built on the patterns of caretaker and victim to understand how each person's opportunity to develop a soul-hearted relationship with themselves is diminished by the patterns of their partner. Michael and Sarah had been married for two years when they came to me for a consultation. They complained that they had been unsatisfied with their relationship periodically over the last seven years and didn't know how to transform it. Throughout their courtship and marriage, Sarah had fulfilled the role of caretaker with Michael, asking little in return. She felt that he took her and their relationship for granted and was tired of setting aside her needs while attending to everyone else's, especially Michael's.

Michael depended on Sarah to take care of him. He considered her his anchor, providing him with security he had never known in his life, without which he felt adrift and incomplete. Several times he had wanted to separate but found it easier to stay in an unfulfilling relationship than to sever his comfortable support system and be alone.

Michael's insecurity stemmed from patterns he had developed in early childhood, with an alcoholic mother and abandoned by his father. Even though he had been raised by a loving and devoted aunt, he continued to seek the love, security, and stability of a parental figure in later relationships. He simply didn't trust that he was lovable, capable, and powerful on his own without a partner to provide such qualities for him.

Sarah's need to rescue others, especially men, had been an inherited family legacy. As a child, Sarah had become a maternal surrogate for her siblings, stepping into this parental role after her father had left following her parents' divorce. In her caregiver role, she had become a master at providing what everyone around her needed but eventually realized that, as a result, she had given up her own needs and dreams.

In the beginning, Sarah had filled Michael's need for a parental figure perfectly, but over time Michael became more resentful of his victim role, while Sarah had become increasing frustrated with deferring her own needs and dreams. Then, during one of our sessions Michael announced that he didn't love Sarah anymore and wanted a divorce. At first Sarah was devastated, although she knew on some level that the relationship had been over for years. It would take her a while to let go of her anger and not view the divorce as abandonment or indicative of personal failure but a cocreated ending to an experience that both she and Michael had manifested. I suggested they try to perceive the situation from each other's point of view and honor their togetherness by beginning to release the relationship with unconditional love.

**To build healthy relationships, we must be fully accountable for recognizing and releasing our patterns. Although this is often difficult to do, it is the only way to free relationships from the parasitic patterns that drain them of the energy they need to thrive and grow. Facing the source of our patterns liberates us from coaddictive situations and allows us to accept full responsibility for creating a new reality that can become a foundation for a soul-hearted relationship with ourselves and eventually a partner.**

PRACTICING THE PRINCIPLES IN CHAPTER THREE

1. *Visualize nature's patterns as a metaphor for your own patterns and life cycles.* Observe the beauty of natural patterns and cycles, noting parallels in your own life, to appreciate how physical existence is based on patterns. Witness a magnificent sunset, walk outside in the falling leaves, or look out the window at the gently falling snow.

2. *Identify and record the negative mindsets, beliefs, and behavioral patterns that interfere with your well-being.* Without judgment, jot down in your journal any negative thoughts and feelings as they surface, even if you are unaware of their significance or source.

3. *Use any uncomfortable feelings that arise, such as pain or fear, to recognize negative patterns and determine their source.* Trace your personal history, including your family legacy, to the sources of negative behavioral patterns that still govern your behavior. Journal to examine how such patterns developed by identifying situations when they first occurred, as well as what types of people and circumstances trigger them in the present. To determine the roots of these patterns, ask yourself the following questions: "In what situations and with what types of people are my physical and emotional reactions most charged?" "Are these reactions caused by my patterns or another person's?" "Under what past circumstances were these patterns formed?" "Do I have

any unfinished business related to them, such as forgiving my family of origin?" Also consider discussing your insights with a trusted therapist or supportive friend.

4. *Observe the cyclical nature of your behavioral patterns.* Write down in your journal repeated occasions when similar patterns have surfaced. Try to identify their triggers by paying attention to the circumstances that prompted them.

5. *Recognize the coaddictive patterns in your relationships.* Become aware of your personal needs and focus on ways to fulfill them yourself, without expecting others to. To identify coaddictive patterns in a relationship, ask yourself: "What needs am I wanting another person to fulfill for me?" "Do I want to feel needed?" "Does being in an exclusive relationship make me feel secure?" "Does my fear of being alone contribute to remaining in an unhealthy relationship?"

6. *Distinguish between your patterned identity and your true being.* To differentiate your patterned identity from your true being, write down as many ways to identify yourself as you can think of, focusing on external characteristics such as "My name is . . . therefore I am," "I think . . . therefore I am," "I believe . . . therefore I am," "My work is . . . therefore I am," "My parents are . . . therefore I am," "My car is . . . therefore I am," or " My body is . . . therefore I am." Then write down as many ways to identify your true being as possible, using positive affirmations such as "I am light; therefore I am," "I am love; therefore I am," "I cocreate life; therefore I am," "I am divine energy; therefore I am." Finally, write the second group of affirmations on Post-it notes and place them where you can see them on a regular basis.

# Chapter Four

## RELEASING PATTERNS AND UNRESOLVED GRIEVANCES

"If you can face and understand your ultimate death,
perhaps you can learn to face and deal productively
with each change that presents itself in your life."

—ELISABETH KÜBLER-ROSS

RELEASING UNHEALTHY BEHAVIORAL PATTERNS and unresolved grievances supports the lifelong development of soul-hearted partnership with ourselves and others. Letting go of such negativity unleashes the flow of positive energy needed for personal transformation and greater selectivity in our relationship choices. It also liberates us to live beyond the superficial, self-destructive roles we play on a daily basis and allows us to express our true being. Many people hide behind the facade of their identity structure and past conditioning, afraid that if they let their guard down they will lose control or be confronted with who they truly are. But it is essential to see that identity structures only offer the illusion of security. And they do not allow us either to adapt to change without becoming uncentered or to use change as a catapult to personal transformation.

Too often we brace ourselves for change instead of letting go of our identity structure and embracing change as an opportunity for personal transformation. In resisting change, however, we actually generate more energy around our insecurities, drawing toward us what we fear most. Playing victim to circumstances, we close our hearts and inhibit the flow of energy that can heal the fragmentation we feel. Then validating our past as a survivor only supports this victim identity, causing us to become mired in misery. But when we open our hearts, we can lean into our fears and insecurities and peel away our identity structure, revealing our true being.

*Peeling Away the Layers of Patterns*

Personal transformation, which prepares us for the shared experience of soul-hearted partnership, necessitates continuously peeling away the layers of our patterns. Like an onion or the Turkish pastry baklava, with its fragile phyllo dough layers, the subtle layers of our patterns must be peeled away on an ongoing basis. We constantly generate life experiences that reveal the next layer of patterns to peel away, a process that occurs throughout our lives and is essential to our physical, emotional, and spiritual growth. Using conscious awareness to recognize the layers of our fear-based patterns gives us the power to step outside of any situation, no matter how difficult or uncomfortable, and release our destructive reactions.

This healthy clearing process is like skin sloughing off dead cells that accumulate and block the growth of new cells. Animals, birds, and plants also move through a regenerative clearing process—cycles of shedding, molting, or loss of leaves—as a part of their natural development. Similarly, as we peel away layers of patterns, we develop a spiritual clarity that transcends our identity structure. When we recognize and release patterns as they surface, we can direct our creative energies toward shaping a more fulfilling life.

The following story about a client, Nicole, illustrates how to use conscious awareness to recognize and release patterns that block our ability to manifest the life and relationships we want. When Nicole was forty-five, she came to a turning point in her life following the death of her mother and realized it was time to enter therapy to explore why she felt depressed. She also wanted to break free of behavioral patterns that had imprisoned her mother and now herself in a series of unfulfilling relationships.

As a child, Nicole became the caretaker of her younger siblings whenever her mother was hospitalized for paranoid schizophrenia and her father was on the road making sales calls. Nicole had also intervened when her mother was at home exhibiting unpredictable behavior such as arguing with the radio or television, yelling at her or her siblings, or wielding kitchen knives at them. During our sessions Nicole saw that in relationships she had played the role of self-sacrificing caretaker so she could distract herself from pain and loss related to her past. Her need to be needed drove her into the arms of men who needed to be rescued. Making their lives wonderful helped her feel more powerful and in control of her emotions, but she soon developed an identity structure characterized by this pattern. It was no wonder that by her second marriage she still felt adrift and lifeless.

Using a therapeutic tool I had suggested, Nicole finally became aware of her pattern and got in touch with her disappointment at having settled for another unhealthy and unfulfilling relationship. She wrote in her journal: "I have now married the second wrong man. Why do I keep going back to these same relationships? What happened to my hopes and dreams? How did I lose myself?"

With my guidance, Nicole began to realize that she was not listening to the voice of spirit through her heart. Afraid to face the reality of how unhappy she was and that her marriage was over, she had closed her heart and was not accessing the guidance of spirit. She also saw that she had ignored her own needs and completely directed her energies toward her husband and the two children she had given birth to. Once she became aware that her personal needs were as important as those of her family and that the relationship was incompatible with realizing her physical, emotional, and spiritual needs, she was ready to start addressing them by developing a loving relationship with herself. Making a covenant to be true to herself, she resolved to pay attention to her own needs first, even though it created upheaval in her family.

To help Nicole break from the identities of wife, mother, and caretaker that guarded the doorway of her inner being, I suggested she develop a ritual of release, taking time alone in a special place to surrender to the emotional pain she had avoided. I further explained that the more she tried to repress her feelings of sadness and despair, the more pronounced her emotional pain would become. Choosing her favorite corduroy chair as a safe sanctuary symbolizing the trusted space of the self, she performed a personalized ritual of release by sitting still and allowing her pain to surface.

Next, I clarified for her that releasing all her emotional pain wouldn't happen overnight, but with time and patience it would be the key to recovering access to her true being and connection with source. And indeed, over a period of months Nicole reached a point where she couldn't hold back her feelings of sadness and despair. As if standing on an ocean beach, she finally faced the turbulent waves of hurt rolling up from within her. At first she felt the undertow of the feelings pull her down until she could no longer breathe. But after surfacing again, she felt as if a weight had been lifted off her heart.

Soon after, I pointed out to Nicole that the series of relationships in which she had felt that something was missing represented a progression toward ultimately having a fulfilling life partner—that rather than failing in her relationships she was actually moving toward the relationship she truly desired. I guided her to see that in her first marriage she had produced a beautiful son and emerged with the qualities of security and loving devotion so she could not consider it a "failed" relationship. But unfortunately she had then become involved too quickly in another exclusive relationship without having first developed and sustained a fuller relationship with herself.

I then helped her see that her second marriage had satisfied her need for spiritual growth, afforded her the opportunity to recognize and release her patterns of insecurity, self-sacrifice, control, and caretaking, and brought the gift of her daughter. She explained that she had chosen to stay in the marriage because she couldn't justify what her friends and family would perceive as another "failed marriage" and also felt a loyalty to remain in the marriage for her children's sake. As it turned out, the factors overriding her heart's desire to leave the marriage were her unresolved feelings about her parents' divorce and her father's subsequent remarriage and divorce. Before she could let go of her current marriage, she had to come to terms with the promise she had made to herself that she would never put her children through this experience.

Eventually, Nicole realized that she had always had the option to choose beyond what her mindsets dictated. She had detoured from her true being's path, making choices out of fear. She thought such choices would satisfy her, but she discovered that they made her feel stagnant and depressed. Once aware of the source of her unhappiness, she became empowered to change those elements of her life that were no longer appropriate to her true being.

Amidst the distractions and fast pace of our lives, we don't always notice the layers of patterns we carry since they can be disguised as anger, annoyance, or discomfort. But we can remember that spiritual tools are available to assist us whenever we deviate from the path of our true being. Like the jack we keep in the trunk of the car in case of a flat tire, these tools are within reach whenever we need them. And they operate like a cosmic cow catcher in front of a locomotive, clearing the track of anything that blocks the forward momentum of our lives.

Using our cosmic cow catcher, we can catch and release negative patterns. Bryan Christopher suggests that one such tool, useful in clearing any fear-based thought, mindset, or belief that crops up, is the mantra "Bless and release"—to be followed by a positive affirmation such as "Don't go there" or "Break the pattern." Give yourself permission to evaluate situations and support the release of reactions rooted in fear.

Another useful tool that can help release patterns, as well as address unresolved grievances and let go of unfulfilling relationships, is a self-designed ritual of release. Examples of rituals of release that I have used myself and suggested to my clients follow.

One ritual of release that I used to resolve my relationship with my mother, who abandoned me when I was young, involved fashioning then burying a miniature time capsule in the form of a coffee can that contained items connected to our relationship. A year-long search for my mother after her twenty-six year absence—a quest that revealed past experiences of loss and pain—ended at the run-down apartment in Pittsburgh where I had last lived with her. I had with me the coffee can containing a photograph that captured my essence at age eight, the year my mother had left me, along with a letter to that little girl expressing my unconditional love for her. I had written: "Dear Debbie, you are a strong, loving, and courageous woman. You are whole and complete light. This is how you came into the world and this is how you will leave. Remember, you have not been abandoned. I have always been there with you. You have blessed and released your painful past. Now, be free to live and express the light of your being." These ritual objects acknowledged both who I was then and who I had become.

I buried the coffee can in the backyard of the apartment building, symbolizing the clearing of patterns and unresolved grief related to my mother. As a result of releasing patterns and forgiving the past, I began to claim my true being so I could create a more positive and fulfilling life.

Another effective ritual of release is one created by a client named Ellen. For years after the death of her mother and grandmother, Ellen had kept some of their clothes, struggling to decide what to do with them. Finally, to release her feelings of grief over her loss of these pivotal women in her life, Ellen made a beautiful quilted pillow using red calico fabric from her grandmother's housedress and blue printed cloth from a dress her mother had worn.

Sewing the squares of the pillow gave her an opportunity to experience emotions and memories related to the women and transform her pain into a new creative undertaking. As she stitched together the cloth fragments, she also was able to integrate the fragmented pieces of herself. Ultimately, she produced a stunning creation that transformed her unresolved grief into a memorable expression of the love she had for these women.

Other rituals of release include making a picture scrapbook, using old photos in a collage about the past, and journaling. Such rituals transform energy held in patterns and unresolved grievances into positive creative experiences. For example, to release her lifelong pattern of victim, another client, Jackie, took photos from her childhood, colored textured papers, and inspired quotes and created a visual journal that depicted her self-healing from child sexual abuse.

Learning how to peel away layers of patterns assists us in embarking on the life we have always envisioned. Instead of becoming aggravated each time we meet up with obstruction, we can clear the track of patterns that no longer serve us and see beyond the illusions of identity structure to our true self and soul potential.


## Forgiving the Past

To forgive our past, we first have to face and resolve any unfinished business from our past choices. This means every pattern and grievance must be examined, like turning over river stones, without hiding behind the facade of excuses. Then, to attain closure, in addition to spiritually releasing our patterns it is also necessary to clean up any physical residue associated with them by getting rid of emotionally charged possessions or gifts, closing bank accounts, changing titles on properties, and letting go of old wedding rings. A memorable scene in the movie *Harold and Maude* depicts Maude achieving physical closure by taking off her wedding ring and throwing it into the water.

Releasing the layers of patterns is a lifelong process because their residue never completely goes away; instead, the layers become subtler and more difficult to discern. Even when we eliminate a pattern, the brain continues to show us a phantom of it. Like a file that we have deleted from our hard drive, its energy as a virtual hologram can still surface physically, alerting us to the past and reminding us to stay true to ourselves. Fortunately, we can reduce its charge by acknowledging our awareness of it, saying, whenever it surfaces, "Hello, pattern, here you are again" and perceiving it only as a phantom of the past.

As the residue of old patterns reveals itself to us, it can prompt us to free ourselves from the past. For example, my second husband and I shared an account number with a grocery store incentive program to earn points toward free gas. As I stopped for gas one afternoon seven years after our divorce, I tried to use my card as always, only to learn that the points in my account had been recently redeemed. Thinking the card had been stolen, I called the customer service manager, who proceeded to explain that the account had been accessed by my ex-husband. It soon dawned on me that this experience offered me an opportunity to forgive the past and clean up the unfinished business from my second marriage by taking my name off the account.

To move forward, it is imperative to clear our lives of anyone or anything that does not align with our vision of future health and happiness. Because residue of patterns can be lurking anywhere in our physical environment, it is necessary to thoroughly evaluate our surroundings for old items inappropriate to our true being that may be blocking our energy. For example, if you open a desk drawer and see papers, photos, or gifts from a previous relationship, regard it as a cue to keep anything you cherish and discard the rest. As if holding an open house at a residence for sale, it is beneficial to set a date for inspecting your living quarters to evaluate your belongings, deciding which items to keep, move to a different place, or release and eliminate.

The following scenario illustrates one woman's approach to completing a relationship and forgiving the past. After the dissolution of her marriage, Ruth, a young accountant, cleared everything out of her life that related to her marriage and wasn't in alignment with developing a healthy relationship with herself. This was the impetus for her to clean out her closets, give away household items that had any connection to the marriage, and move everything else that didn't resonate with her out of her house. Finally, forgiving her past, she changed her last name and had the new name put on the title of her house, thereby taking charge of her new life as a single woman in full partnership with herself.

Ruth's family and friends waited for the other shoe to drop as she cleaned up the residue of her relationship. Believing that her head was in the clouds and her feet were not on the ground, they were certain she was making a mistake, that she would fail to survive as a single woman and would have to sell her house, close her accounting practice, and go back to her ex-husband. They supported the same fear-based myths she had heard all her life, such as "People need to stay in a relationship at all costs" and "It is impossible to reach for the stars and fulfill your dreams."

In our sessions, Ruth discovered the value of trusting her own experience and consistently making choices with clarity, despite resistance from other people in her life. Realizing she was doing nothing wrong by following her heart, she began to release her patterns of insecurity and seeking approval. Instead of acquiescing to the conditional support of her family and friends, she learned to trust the unconditional love she was developing for herself, which gave her the courage to transform her life. Even though

Ruth was undergoing a tumultuous transition, she knew she had taken charge in a way she never had before. As she continued to make discerning choices regarding things that now worked for her, she began to feel an inner security she hadn't felt since her childhood. Once her life began to flourish, her family and friends were shocked, but she knew the transformation was because she trusted her ability to make her own dreams come true.

My client Linda had an equally interesting experience completing a relationship and forgiving the past. Twenty-two years after she and her first husband were divorced, he invited her to breakfast without first telling her why he wanted to meet with her. Linda graciously accepted his invitation. As they were sitting at the table reflecting on their terrific son, her ex gazed at her, took a deep breath, and said, "The main reason I wanted to meet today was to share with you that I'm an alcoholic." He proceeded to tell her he had recently completed a chemical dependency treatment program and now wanted to make amends for not having been present in their relationship, as well as take full responsibility for his part in their breakup. Stunned while listening to his words, she became intensely aware of the need to complete her pattern of caretaker during the marriage, and together they forgave the past.

While it is possible to temporarily "slip" and get entangled once again in the residue of patterns, we have to trust the voice of spirit to guide us in completing patterns and forgiving the past. When we embrace this natural shedding rather than resisting it, we release additional patterns that no longer serve us, gradually exposing more of our true being. This process leads to a new beginning and a spiritual awakening.

*Embracing Transitions As Periods of Transformation*
Transitions—intense periods of discovery, self-healing, and personal transformation—can catalyze the release of patterns, the resolution of grievances, and open space for new possibilities and spiritual growth. From a spiritual point of view, a person's life is a constant series of transitions: changing jobs or careers, suffering from and healing an illness, beginning or ending relationships, having a baby or facing a death in the family, and initiating or completing creative projects.

Although these transitions may make us feel that we are losing our bearings, they are actually signs that we are processing new and stored information simultaneously and expanding our conscious awareness. They can also be seen as times of gathering strength physically, mentally, and spiritually in preparation for the next step forward in life—just as it is necessary to spring up at the end of a diving board to gather momentum for a full twist into the pool.

While moving through transitions, we may experience physical and emotional exhaustion, anxiety, and disorientation. Releasing past patterns and absorbing new information blows the circuits of the brain as it sorts through stored files trying to make sense of the new data coming in through the heart. At such times we might get confused and start misplacing items, bumping into walls, or dropping fragile articles. I get lost driving to places I know, careen into furniture, and even forget where I am. Fortunately, now that I am aware of what transitions feel like I no longer confuse them with early dementia, as I once did.

During a transition, we need to slow down and center ourselves, be aware of all that is happening around us, and remain true to ourselves and our vision for the future. To ground ourselves during such stressful periods when everything is in flux, we can breathe deeply; touch the center of the chest and open the heart; take a walk or work in the garden, using the elements of nature to calm us; or bathe to cleanse our energy field.

An experience a few years ago reminded me that transitions are often initiated when spirit brings in new information to prepare us for the future. My husband, Doug, had presented me with a stunning, blue-violet tanzanite ring for my forty-seventh birthday while we were on vacation in Panama. Because we were traveling out of the country and needed to keep the ring safe, we affectionately started calling it "Precious."

Six months later, I stopped by the jewelry store and had the ring cleaned while I waited. As soon as they were finished, I immediately placed the ring back on my finger, put on my leather glove, and left the store. When I arrived home, I took off my glove to admire the sparkling ring and noticed a small hairline crack inside the stone. As the day went on, the crack grew larger until it looked like the stone had shattered inside.

Doug and I called the jeweler and our insurance company to ask about our options for replacing the stone. Trusting that what was happening was not to upset but to inform me, with conscious awareness I observed the replacement process and contemplated the meaning of the incident for my life. First, the jeweler offered to replace the stone without any further charge to us. Then our insurance company sent a check to the jeweler to cover the cost of a new stone. Witnessing everything, I became convinced that the stone had imploded from the inside out as a spiritual sign of a powerful transition to come. My intuition was affirmed two weeks later when I had a suspicious mammogram that began a year-long process of self-healing and personal transformation.

The metamorphosis of the piece of jewelry ultimately foreshadowed another important transition in my life. First, I was led to replace the old stone with something new to symbolize letting go of the past and opening to the future. When the jeweler brought out a deep blue sapphire stone for me to examine, I chose it as a symbolic declaration for my future. Six months later, unbeknownst to me, my husband bought the damaged tanzanite stone from the jeweler, had it sent to a gem cutter in California, and on my forty-eighth birthday presented me with a beautiful tanzanite necklace. It was "Precious" transformed into two stones, a heart and a triangle joined together on top. Little did I know at the time that these two shapes would become the symbols for soul-hearted partnership, a concept I would channel for my book within the next year.

The following are ways to remain positive and centered while moving through intense transitions. First, regard such shifts as natural life occurrences, seeing parallels in the natural world. Viewing transitions as natural allows us to act in ways that direct more of our creative energies into new possibilities for our future. For example, aware that you will be selling your house in the near future, you can refrain from investing time or money in building an addition and instead make repairs and continue keeping it beautiful so you can still enjoy it. Similarly, you can let go of relationships that tie you to the past and are no longer appropriate for your life, while sustaining the others through healthy detachment and unconditional love.

Also, we can clear potential energy blocks so that we remain an open channel of creative energy. Just as water runs through a hose when it is open and free of kinks, so does energy flow freely when there are no energy blocks due to unresolved negativity, resistance, or avoidance. So be sure to release any pattern of resistance or avoidance, which may otherwise only intensify your transition and in some cases produces a physical, emotional, or financial crisis.

Energy blocks can be produced by any toxicity in an environment. The blocks occur within the body, which is impacted, whether we are conscious of it or not, by all thoughts, feelings, and habits. Even the choices we make to live in a specific location or work at a particular job affect the flow of our energy.

Energy blocks can also develop when there is someone or something in our environment with which we do not resonate, such as a couch that is not aligned with our true being. When we clutter our environment with people or things that are inappropriate to our true being, we drain our physical energy, which generates stagnancy and illness.

An example of how the removal of energy blocks releases new potential occurs in the following story about a client named Lynn. Every time Lynn walked into her master bedroom, her grandmother's rocking chair grabbed her attention. She recalled the day when her mother had given her the heirloom chair and how she felt obligated to take it. Unlike her mother, who adored this antique, she had never resonated with its design or meaning. Consequently, she had placed it in the corner of her bedroom and covered it with discarded clothing, but it was still a drain on her energies because it was a constant reminder of the dubious choice she had made to accept something she didn't want. Finally recognizing this, Lynn found a friend who adored the quaint rocking chair and moved it to her home. This choice freed her creative energies so that she could manifest an intention more appropriate to her true being, such as a new bed she desired.

When we block the flow of energy and thus the guidance of spirit through the heart, we upset our chemical and metabolic systems, weakening the immune system or causing depression or disease. It is therefore essential to release them on a regular basis, restoring balance to the physical, mental, and emotional systems.

The more we clear energy blocks, caused by accumulations of people and things related to our former lives, the more the flow of energy becomes available to create new potential. Moving through life from one transition to another without resistance, avoidance, or energy blocks allows us to open to these new possibilities and develop spiritually.


*Entering the Space of Vulnerability*
The space of vulnerability is the place where we confront ourselves alone, stripped of our patterns and defenses. In this space, the ego begins to step aside, the chatter of the mind lessens, and we get in touch with our true being. There follows a silent dialogue with ourselves that can kindle a purification in the midst of what otherwise feels like a spiritual crisis.

Initially, being alone can make us feel anxious, yearning for the identity structure we have long relied on; fortunately, we need not stay in this space more than ten minutes, though a longer duration may improve the results. Such solitude can cause waves of emotion to surface like ocean swells crashing onto the shore, and we can lose our balance as when an undertow pulls us below the surface. Letting out our gut-wrenching pain allows us to feel more fully. Yet despite such intense feelings, we can persist in the space of vulnerability by reminding ourselves that it will allow us to see and uproot patterns that inhibit full self-expression. In witnessing our internal processes, we become aware of how our negative thoughts can trigger a chain reaction of emotions, such as fear, sadness, or disappointment. We also discover that our anxiety, grievances, and other problems derive from external sources.

When our fears and insecurities are revealed and released in the space of vulnerability, we may feel like Humpty Dumpty falling off a wall and shattering into pieces. It's likely we will grieve the loss of the false security provided by our patterns and defense mechanisms. But once we move through this experiential death, we see that only our identity structure has died, not our true being. In fact, we must allow our identity structure to die so that we can experience what it feels like to be fully alive.

The story of my client Elise is a good example of this type of experiential death. Thirty years after her mother had died, Elise, at age thirty-eight, returned to Ireland to visit her family and her mother's gravesite. Spending time with her family opened up a flood of unresolved feelings of loss and activated painful flashbacks to her childhood. Near the end of her visit, as Elise and her younger sister had lunch on a pier watching the fishing trawlers dock, her sister shared an experience of a close friend who had purposely walked into the sea and drowned. Listening to her sister, Elise felt overwhelmed with sadness and knew that she, too, could commit suicide by walking into the ocean.

After returning home, Elise felt swept up in an emotional tsunami of depression. She tried desperately to hold the fragments of herself together, fearful that without a grip on herself she would die. The more she resisted grieving, however, the closer she felt to death, suffering from heart palpitations and chronic lung disease.

One beautiful May day, suicide became a viable option for stopping the pain she felt. In preparation, she set a bottle of Irish whiskey and sleeping pills on the kitchen table. Then, as she contemplated her choice, a gas company employee knocked on the door wanting to read her meter. At that moment, she felt as if she had been resuscitated by electrical paddles.

I met Elise following her suicide attempt. Since visiting her family the year before, she had been steadily unraveling and having vivid dreams that her mother's spirit was with her. Then during her job working with hospice patients, the husband of a patient had played music that Elise recognized as one of her mother's favorite pieces, an incident that made her realize she had been ignoring intuitive messages. This awakening led to her release of unresolved losses and healing.

As Elise's story exemplifies, the loss of a significant relationship, even one characterized by distress, if left unresolved can produce separation anxiety and a sense of fragmentation of the self. Without letting go of these losses, we can have difficulty moving from one transition to another, a passage that brings about physical, emotional, and spiritual maturation.

Despite the pain it elicits, loss teaches us about the delicate balance, intensity, and richness of life, for we cannot experience the pain of loss without first having experienced the joys associated with what has been lost. In the movie *Shadowlands*, the poet Joy Gresham, in speaking about her impending death to author C. S. Lewis, who late in life savored the delights of romance and passion with her, says, "The greater the love, the deeper the sorrow—and the longer it will take to work through it. That's the deal."[1]

Grieving our losses by embracing emotional vulnerability is the path to healing our fractured self and expressing our fullest potential. Losses we suffer can derive from a wide range of situations. Author and journalist Judith Viorst points out, "[When we think of loss,] we think of the loss through death of people we love. Loss, however, is a far more encompassing theme in our life. For we lose not only through death but also by leaving and being left, by changing and moving on. And our losses include not only our separations and departures from those we love, but our conscious and unconscious losses of romantic dreams, impossible expectations, illusions of freedom and power, illusions of safety, and the loss of our younger self, the self that thought it always would be unwrinkled, invulnerable, and immortal."[2]

The act of blessing and releasing anyone or anything assists us in forgiving our past, allows us to better appreciate the present, and orients us toward the future. And forgiving our past permits us to embrace our natural life cycles, accepting life as a series of births and deaths, transitions that lead to personal transformation. Entering the space of vulnerability to dissolve our identity structure and access our true being allows us to experience the other side of fear, which is love and trust in ourselves. The surge of creative energy derived from this love and trust empowers us to manifest a new life of endless possibilities.

*Blessing and Releasing Unhealthy and Unfulfilling Relationships*

Maintaining unhealthy and unfulfilling relationships can drain our life force, while letting go of them empowers us to shift our reality and create space for new relationships that enhance our spiritual growth. Blessing and releasing unhealthy and unfulfilling relationships with unconditional love and integrity can teach us how to forgive our past, heal ourselves, and generate positive energy to progress on our spiritual path toward greater growth and fulfillment. If we do not break clean from an unhealthy relationship and stop investing energy in it, we will continue to desperately keep it alive while knowing in our hearts that our spirit has already left it, causing us to feel dead inside.

Many relationships come to a pivotal point where one person has grown to such a degree that the other partner must transform as well or the relationship will be in jeopardy. Usually the partner resists the natural shift that is occurring by creating distraction or drama, which ignites tension and conflict. At this crossroads, one or both partners may choose to end the relationship or use the creative energy that has been awakened to transform the relationship.

While working with couples, I often ask each person at the beginning of the session, "How do you think things are going with your relationship?" Many times one partner will tell me they think things are good and they feel close to their partner, while the other person discloses that they want a separation or divorce. On the other hand, in some cases both partners may be able to move through the crisis by letting go of the old form of their relationship and cocreating a new form capable of sustaining mutual spiritual growth.

Blessing and releasing unhealthy and unfulfilling relationships is often challenging. For one thing, there is the matter of loyalty or fear of not finding another relationship. Even when we know it is in our best interest to let go of someone we loved and move on, thoughts of doing so trigger upheaval, such as feelings of guilt, resentment, anger, disappointment, or sadness. This is especially true if the partners are in different stages of emotional or spiritual growth or if they disagree about terminating the relationship. One may feel ready to release the relationship, while the other person, terrified of change, is adamantly holding on to it. In this scenario, one partner will stop at nothing to block the ending of the relationship, resistance that causes conflict and prevents healing. As a result, much energy is spent on judging and blaming, which only produces more complications in ending the relationship.

In addition, many people are influenced by the myth that the passionate, divine union of souls they envision as their ideal is an unattainable dream or a perfect script for a movie. Consequently, they convince themselves that their relationship is "as good as it gets" and settle for a facsimile of soul-hearted partnership.

Society itself encourages people to remain in unfulfilling relationships by perpetuating the myth that you should "stay and work it out" or "remain loyal to the family" even when the relationship is supporting self-destructive patterns or is incompatible with the partners' emotional or spiritual needs. But when families and friends support the status quo they are usually motivated, either consciously or unconsciously, by the desire to keep their own lives unaffected by changes resulting from the breakup, especially financial or emotional burdens. When partners yield to such societal demands to remain in unhealthy and unfulfilling relationships, they sacrifice their individual dreams, which ultimately stifles their spiritual growth.

Also, if people doing inner spiritual work contemplate leaving an unfulfilling relationship, they often procrastinate, ignoring unmistakable signs and experiences that tell them the relationship's life cycle has ended. To create a new, deeper relationship, they must completely release patterns associated with the former one and enter into a spiritual covenant with each other to transform their partnership.

In preparing to bless and release an unhealthy or unfulfilling relationship, it is first important to remember that the demise of the relationship cannot be blamed on one partner. The old adage "It takes two to tango" holds true because each person is accountable for the direction the relationship has taken regardless of who is dissolving it. When both people take full responsibility for every choice in their lives, including being in the relationship in the first place, then there are no victims, and peaceful coexistence is possible.

When both people take responsibility for cocreating and letting go of their relationship, they validate the purpose the relationship has served and their experiences in it. Here is an example of such an acknowledgment in the form of a letter one person wrote to their ex-partner expressing appreciation and love: "My dear one, let us always remember the purpose that brought us together and that we entered into our relationship with meaningful intention, support, and love. Let us now part in love and appreciation for each other. I release our relationship for my own spiritual transformation and hold you in the sacredness of my heart forever. Together, let's declare a new positive intention to separate well in love, care, and mutual understanding."

There are several ways to evaluate whether an unhealthy and unfulfilling relationship is worth keeping and working on or if it is so dependent on history and patterns, and so fraught with incompatibilities that we need to terminate and release it. One way is to ask ourselves: "Is this relationship appropriate to my true being and for this period of my life?" This question implies that we are in touch with our true being and can assess whether the relationship is supporting it. Talking with a therapist or journaling can assist us in determining which aspects of the relationship may be at odds with our true being and spiritual growth.

Another way to evaluate whether a relationship supports our personal well-being and growth is to ask ourselves: "Does this relationship affirm and enhance my well-being?" "Does this person love, trust, and support me with integrity?" and "Do I feel good about myself when I am with this person?" If the answers are yes, then it is worth maintaining the relationship. If the answers are maybe, observe more and remain in touch with the person for the time being. If the answers are no, bless and release the relationship, wishing the other person a happy life.

When we recognize that a relationship is over and we need to let go, we have to balance between two realities—the physical reality of the relationship and the spiritual reality that our spirit has moved on and is informing us of new future possibilities. Dealing with the physical reality may seem like visiting a gravesite where there remains a physical marker of the deceased while the deceased's spirit has gone elsewhere. It is under such circumstances, where physical remnants of a relationship still exist within the spiritual vacuum, that transitional relationships tend to occur. Although it may be tempting at such a time to "cut and run," it is beneficial to allow time for a healthy, healing breakup. This is because we need to complete the relationship energy and review its significance in our lives to clear the necessary space for eventually cocreating another one or choosing to remain alone.

The following are guidelines for completing a relationship with unconditional love, respect, and integrity. First, give yourself permission to let go of the relationship without experiencing guilt, fear, shame, or hopelessness. Remember, the other person has the power of choice too, even when it looks like they're being left. In releasing the relationship with unconditional love, you give the other person permission to love and leave as well.

Second, trust yourself, listen to your heart, and use your expanded conscious awareness to guide you. Reflect on the purposes for which the relationship was cocreated and how the needs of the partners may have changed. Consider the fact that some relationships can remain intact as partners grow, while others need to be dissolved because the partners must follow their own hearts. Also recognize that relationships can be appreciated as invaluable personal experiences even if they ultimately need to be terminated.

Third, choose a safe and neutral place to communicate your desire to end the relationship as clearly and honestly as possible. Be prepared for angry or hurt reactions from the other person. Take responsibility for your choices and refrain from blaming or judging the other person so you don't fall into the pattern of right versus wrong. Treat yourself and the other person with utmost care and kindness as you work to dissolve the relationship so the experience of it will serve you in a beneficial way as you initiate future relationships in your life.

When a face-to-face conversation with the other person might result in too much conflict, first write a letter or e-mail to ensure clear and honest communication. Express your point of view with "I" statements and accept the other person's perspective without blame or judgment. Then, when you feel ready to talk in person, speak in a loving tone of voice, allow uninterrupted time for each of you to express your views, and immediately stop any conversation that leads to bickering or blaming.

Fourth, allow sufficient time for each partner's adjustment to any changes that result from dissolution of the relationship. Do not presume that the other person is as prepared as you are mentally, emotionally, and spiritually. Decide on a reasonable time line for resolving business, such as sorting personal belongings or joint properties, negotiating living space, re-arranging finances, and untangling family ties and mutual friendships.

Fifth, bless the relationship as you release it, transcending any negativity about the other person or the relationship. One way to do this is to invoke unconditional love and to visualize enveloping the other person with love and light energy. Acknowledge love for your own being, the being of the other person, and the connection shared, while releasing the physical bonds of the relationship. You can use the phrase "Bless and release" as a mantra or prayer to clear your body and mind so that spirit will guide you to let go and open to new possibilities. All the while, trust yourself and your connection to source, acknowledge the reasons you came together in the first place, and honor the purpose the relationship has served. Such an energetic completion allows you to appreciate the other person and simultaneously sustain a relationship with your true self. The intention to bless and release the relationship opens space for both people to transform their lives.

A good tool to use in blessing and releasing a relationship with unconditional love and integrity is a ritual. This worked well for my client Claire. Although she had broken off her relationship with Jack, I encouraged her to tie up loose ends of their partnership by eliminating her pattern of caretaking and shifting her creative energies to caring for herself. To let go of her pattern of caretaking, she stopped answering his abusive calls in the middle of the night, deleted his phone number from her speed dial, and removed his possessions from her apartment. She decided if he wanted closure he would have to arrange an appropriate time and place to meet with her.

Claire then completed the relationship by designing a ritual of release. A few months after breaking up with Jack, she traveled solo to Mexico, aware that she had to face her fear of being alone. Once Claire had enjoyed a few days at the beach, her heart told her it was time to put the past behind her. The next morning, she headed for the beach, walking down a rocky path lined with lilac and sage bushes that filled the air with heavenly scents. At the beach, she dug a hole big enough to bury her experiences of loss associated with every relationship in her life. Next she read aloud the eulogy she had written: "My dear Jack, you gave me the opportunity to witness and love myself. You believed in me and truly loved me—thank you. I will always remember your unique spirit and am grateful for knowing you and the time together. I bless and release you from my life." Then she placed sprigs of sage she had picked on his picture, laid it and the eulogy in the hole, and covered them with sand. Finally, she placed a stone on top of the makeshift grave.

For the first time since she had left the relationship, she felt at peace. She also knew that she was not alone but in touch with her true being and connected to her source, which had always been there. By not settling for an unfulfilling relationship, she opened herself to the possibility of cocreating a fulfilling one with someone else in the future.

Blessing and releasing unhealthy and unfulfilling relationships unleashes a flow of energy through the heart. This energetic validation of partnership with ourselves manifests soul-hearted partnerships with others in the future.

**Releasing patterns and unresolved grievances frees us to discover and support our true being. Then, listening to the voice of spirit through the heart, we are guided to see that we are responsible for cocreating our own reality, and we make more discerning choices for a more fulfilling life.**

## Practicing the Principles in Chapter Four

1. *Examine and forgive your unresolved grievances.* Take a written or verbal inventory of your unresolved grievances and identify your personal wounds by asking yourself these questions: "What past or present memories, situations, or relationships require forgiveness and healing?" "Am I holding on to grievances against others, and am I afraid to let go of them?" "How has harboring resentment against another person or myself interfered with my spiritual growth?"

2. *Use the phrase "Bless and release" as a mantra or prayer for clearing your body, mind, and spirit.* Every time you notice a fear-based thought, feeling, or pattern, think or say, "Bless and release," to dissipate any negative energy or patterns. Alternately, when you notice negativity touch the center of your chest and direct your heart to let go of whatever reaction you are holding. Send light energy out to encircle the person or thing involved and invite your spirit to release the negativity.

3. *Walk consciously through your environment and notice where possible energy blocks exist.* Observe everything and assess whether or not it serves you well and is appropriate for you in your current life circumstances. Clear your house of anyone or anything that does not align with your well-being and future intentions.

4. *Evaluate the appropriateness of your relationships for your current level of spiritual development.* Review the directory in your cell phone to see which relationships support your well-being and your path to self-realization. As you look at the name of each individual, ask, "Does this person support me unconditionally in my life?" and "Does this relationship enrich my life?" If you answer yes to either of these questions, retain their name and number. If you answer no, eliminate them from the directory.

5. *Create a personal ceremony to bless and release any person or pattern that does not resonate with your true being, using items related to the person or pattern or a statement of intent related to a new life in the future.* Possible ceremonies may include a private prayer service, the burning of items, the creation of a picture scrapbook or journal, or the designing of a collage that reflects your future intentions.

# Chapter Five

## COCREATING OUR REALITY
## BY MANIFESTING INTENTIONS

"If one is lucky, a solitary fantasy
can totally transform one million realities."

——MAYA ANGELOU

W E EACH HAVE THE INNATE ABILITY to move beyond our patterns and cocreate a life that resonates with our true being. We begin moving in this direction by recognizing and releasing patterns that block our ability to manifest the reality we most desire. Then, trusting our connection to a divine energy source, we channel its flow of creative energy to help us make choices more aligned with our fullest soul potential. What ultimately helps us develop a fully realized relationship with ourselves and then with a beloved partner is our inherent ability to manifest intentions.

### The Transformative Power of Intention

Like an inspired artist facing a blank canvas, we can use intention to alter the direction of our lives. Intention functions like a cosmic Roto-Rooter, transforming situations or relationships entrenched in deeply rooted patterns by drawing toward us opportunities that are better aligned with the fulfillment of our potential. Intention, when supported by our connection to a divine energy source, sets up the people, places, and opportunities that may shape our future realities. It is then up to us to select from these possibilities choices that align with our true being. The more we learn to trust the power of our intentions, the easier it is to let go of the lives we have had until now and know we can manifest more fulfilling ones.

Most people spend their entire lives accepting what they think are the fixed circumstances of their existence. Despite feeling alone, alienated, and adrift in their situation, they do everything in their power to fit in and avoid personal transformation. Their sense of disconnection and powerlessness drains physical and creative energy and reinforces patterns of futility and avoidance. They find trusting their connection to source difficult and often ignore any spiritual information revealed through their hearts. Consequently, they become bogged down in their daily problems and diminish their ability to transcend seemingly fixed circumstances and channel their creative energy positively.

But no matter how dire our circumstances, we have the inherent ability to transcend the conditions of our lives and shift our reality by using intentions to redirect the flow of our energy. It has often been observed that when individuals react negatively to someone or something, they generate more negativity, while their positive responses produce more vitality and well-being. This means that to generate better outcomes when we become angry, judgmental, or resentful toward people, we can pause, breathe deeply, open our hearts with compassion, and choose instead to bless people or wish them a great day. In this way, we disengage from negative hooks and channel the energy saved toward positive choices. Author Gary Zukav, in his book *The Seat of the Soul*, takes this notion further, writing, "Every experience and every change in your experience reflects intention."[1]

We begin using intention for positive change by knowing in our hearts that this is not just a possibility but a certainty. In directing our energy positively and consciously declaring our intentions, we open ourselves to the energy of cocreation. Like dropping a pebble into a pond, our intention, in cocreation with a divine energy source, sets off an energetic vibration that radiates outward from our heart center and shifts everything in our path, altering the choices we will have in the future.

Next, we need to watch for opportunities that align with our intention and make discerning choices. As Ralph Waldo Emerson poignantly reminds us, once we arrive at a decision the universe conspires to bring it about. For example, if we declare the intention that we want a soul-hearted relationship with a beloved partner, then after preparing by having a soul-hearted relationship with ourselves, as opportunities arise we can make choices that support having such a person show up in our lives. These choices may be difficult, perhaps requiring us to eliminate some of our already established relationships, change where we live or work, use an online dating site, or alter our lifestyle, all in the interest of allowing our energy to flow more freely in manifesting our desires. Nevertheless, we will have the strength to make such changes by trusting in the guidance of spirit.

An example of declaring an intention to shift perspective and direction in life is the following story about a client. Sheila had been in a relationship for ten years, was fifty pounds overweight, and so depressed she barely could get out of bed in the morning. She had found out that the man with whom she was living was cheating on her and decided to leave the unhealthy relationship. To get started, she began focusing on her own physical and emotional health by working out, getting bodywork done, seeing a therapist, and especially running. Like Forrest Gump, Sheila's goal was to run gradually farther and farther—first to the end of the block, then a mile, and ultimately several miles. As a result, she lost weight, became less depressed, and felt more positive about her life. A year later she participated in a marathon. About ten miles into the race, an Aboriginal man ran up next to her and said, "How far do you plan on going?" and she replied, "As far as I can." Then the man said, "It doesn't matter how far you go because you are already there." As she finished, she realized that her intention to run as far as possible had been more crucial to her success than establishing a goal of going a certain distance. After this, she was able to use her intentions to manifest more fulfilling situations that led to a more satisfying relationship with herself and others.

Using the power of intention is not about setting a specific goal and focusing so much on it that you lose sight of other possibilities. On the contrary, it is about setting a goal, being open to the many choices that present themselves in reaching that goal, then selecting the ones most likely to bring about the desired outcome.

Just as a plane is guided onto the runway, into the air, and to its destination by airline personnel and air traffic controllers, you, as copilot, can guide your intention into reality by conavigating with your source. Making your flight plan a reality, however, necessitates being out in front of your intention, which means thinking and acting as if your intention has already manifested. Spirit then manifests your intention by guiding the choices you make. You can be out in front of your intention by using creative visualization. Close your eyes and imagine how your manifested intention would look and feel in your life. Next, trust and affirm that your intention has already been manifested. Then expand your conscious awareness so you are open to the spiritual information that comes through your heart, guiding the choices that bring your intention into reality.

In addition, because any thought or spoken word functions as an intention, it is crucial to keep thoughts and words positive. The phrase "Be careful what you wish for" applies to the potential outcomes of thinking or speaking negatively. If you catch yourself thinking or speak negatively, shift your ideas, words, or tone to be more positive.

It is important that our intentions reflect what we want rather than what we don't want, because any intention has the power to manifest. For instance, if you complain to a coworker that you hate your job and wish you didn't have to be there, you are setting a negative intention. In generating energy to support this intention, you may get your wish and end up being fired. For better results you could express your intention positively by saying, for example, "I want to use my talents and abilities to create a new career" or "I desire a job in which I can express myself more fully." Having set a positive intention, you can manifest a new job by being aware of possibilities that will help you find it, such as talking to someone who tells you about another position, seeing a job advertised in the paper or on the Internet, or running into a friend who wants to start a business with you.

Trusting the manifestation of our intentions transforms our reality and allows us to relinquish attempts to control our destiny, such as trying to physically, mentally, or emotionally manipulate people, thus helping us attain more peace of mind and work more cooperatively with others. The Serenity Prayer used in AA and other self-empowerment programs underscores this dynamic by stressing the advantage of accepting the things we cannot change (such as other people), having the courage to change the things we can (such as ourselves), and having the wisdom to know the difference.

Familiarity with the transformative power of intention makes us realize that we have many more possibilities in life than we could possibly envision through the lens of old mindsets. In cocreating with our divine source, we can consciously choose what we want in life. And with new confidence in the innate power of intention to manifest our desires, we can trust in our ability to make our dreams come true.


*Accepting Responsibility for Manifesting Our Reality*
To manifest a more fulfilling life, we have to accept responsibility for our intentions and the life circumstances they reflect. One way to think of accepting this responsibility is by regarding it as being "response-able"— that is, responding to events instead of reacting to them.

Responding rather than reacting to life requires the perspective necessary to make more enlightened choices, which we can acquire through detachment, or refusing to take things personally and instead listening to the voice of spirit guiding us through the heart. For example, suppose you are ready to leave the house for a scheduled appointment and someone who is going with you is dawdling and not ready to go. You could react by nagging or becoming upset and feeling at the mercy of the other person's choices. Or you could be response-able, communicating your need to be on time, maintaining your sense of humor, and then making a choice with your best interest at heart, trusting that your choice will work well. In the end you may opt to take separate cars, leave for the appointment alone, and meet the other person there without anger or blame; you are fully aware there is no right or wrong, no duty or obligation, only personal responsibility. These actions, prompted by a detached perspective, all demonstrate a response rather than a reaction to the potentially frustrating situation.

In accepting responsibility for our choices in all situations and being response-able, we can circumvent the interactions that get us into self-destructive conflicts. For example, many of us have had the experience of being pulled over by a police officer for a traffic violation. We hear the siren, look in the rearview mirror, and have a sinking feeling inside. At this point, we can be response-able by opening our hearts, confidently pulling over, then, when the officer approaches the car, immediately being accountable for our actions. If we are presented with a ticket, we can graciously accept it and thank the officer for encouraging us to slow down, affirming that we energetically set up the intervention as an incentive to take better care of ourselves. Finally, we can view the situation as an opportunity to pay closer attention to our well-being.

The willingness to take responsibility for our circumstances prepares us to take charge and be flexible in any situation, from getting a traffic ticket to experiencing a flight delay, or any other sudden change in plans. Then, instead of expecting the worst, we respond with trust that everything is working out for the best and openness to whatever information the situation might offer. To support this foundation of trust, we need only recall similar incidents we endured without major problems and possibly better outcomes.

The following example illustrates the significance of taking responsibility for our happiness and well-being while in a relationship. Although Mark was a confident and successful attorney, he had always lived his life in a state of anxiety and insecurity. Because early in his life he had experienced perpetual chaos in his home and had felt abandoned by his parents, he operated in his adult life as if he had no control. His lack of trust in himself and in his ability to manifest a wonderful life immobilized him in his work, marriage, and social life. He felt trapped in his marriage but was terrified to dissolve it. Stuck in his pattern of avoiding action, he remained on the fence, waiting for his wife Susan to leave him. In doing this, he was unconsciously recreating his childhood pattern of avoidance and abandonment.

I assisted Mark in recognizing that by avoiding ending his marriage, he was abdicating his responsibility for changing his life. Ironically, by waiting for Susan to initiate the needed change, he was still making a choice, but one based on fear, without taking responsibility.

Although we, like Mark, may resist accepting responsibility for our choices because it seems easier to relinquish our power to fear, in doing so we forfeit the opportunity to cocreate our reality. Being accountable for everything in our life is the key to personal freedom. And when we take full responsibility for our choices, refusing to blame others for them, we can be response-able even in the most challenging, life-altering circumstances and attract everyone and everything we need to manifest a more fulfilling reality.

## Making Our Dreams a Reality

The power of choice allows us to make our dreams a reality through the energy of creation. We cocreate our reality by declaring our intentions and channeling energy positively to make responsible choices that align with our hearts' desires. Like stepping stones across a stream, it often takes a series of choices to manifest our intentions. Therefore, we must always be willing to let go of original choices when they are no longer appropriate to our true being, and make new choices that will result in fulfilling our soul potential.

Like combing the beach for special shells, we have to discover then sort through a myriad of possibilities before making a final choice. When we are attracted to a particular shell, we pick it up, examine it, and decide whether or not it resonates with us. If it does, we save it, and if it doesn't we toss it back on the beach. As new shells appear, we might substitute some of them for those we have saved. We continue this sorting process until we finish our walk and decide which shells to take home. Similarly, we have to sort through numerous choices every day to select those that align with our hearts' desires and then let go of the rest.

At times, the sequence of choices that lead to making dreams a reality may appear random, but we have to trust the voice of spirit speaking through the heart that there is a spiritual purpose to the chain of selections, which reflects divine synchronicity. Divine synchronicity occurs when we empower ourselves to move beyond fear and self-doubt, declare intentions, and use positive energy to manifest them. During such experiences, we feel like a conduit for the spiritual information moving us toward manifesting our intentions. As such, we will know when our next choice appears and how to implement it.

The following story is an example of such divine synchronicity. My client Valerie's niece, Lea, and husband, Bill, moved in with her after their house burned down in San Diego. Ironically, prior to the fire Lea and Bill's relationship had died out and they had been considering a separation, but following the fire they decided to stay together and rebuild. A year later, however, Lea was diagnosed with fourth-stage lung cancer and passed away.

After Lea died, Bill was saddened and longed to find another partner for a fulfilling relationship. One night, he woke up from a dream and, seemingly out of the blue, remembered a woman he and Lea had known twenty years before, while living in another neighborhood. Following this clue, he went back to the neighborhood and, trusting his heart, left a note on the woman's gatepost. The woman subsequently decided to contact Bill, and eventually they began living happily together. Although these choices seemed random, they actually occurred because Bill was guided by spirit to make choices that manifested his intention to have a new partner.

Another example of apparently random choices aligning with intention is the following tale. In gratitude for hosting her bridal shower, Laura gave her mother a fifty-dollar bill, knowing that she enjoyed playing the Lucky Leprechaun nickel slot machines at the casino. With nothing on her calendar the next morning, her mother drove to a new casino and sat down at a Lucky Leprechaun nickel slot that caught her attention. Before playing the machine, she declared her intention: to win enough money to host a brunch the day after Laura's wedding for the out-of-town guests. Then she put the fifty-dollar bill into the machine and on the third spin, Lucky Leprechaun flew out saying, in his Irish brogue, "You have the highest number combination possible." She had won $563.00 just enough to host the wedding brunch. Such experiences of divine synchronicity become more common when we act on "pure thoughts" that seem to come out of the blue, with no connection to an agenda.

The opportunity to constantly make new choices empowers us to be proactive in shaping our life circumstances. By declaring our intentions and following our hearts, we open ourselves to the possibility of divine synchronicity. And by being a conduit for information from spirit that guides our choices, we become active cocreators of a fulfilling future.

## Choices That Invite Miracles

Choices that invite miracles are those that dramatically alter our perspective, manifest something beyond what we ever thought possible, and either present a crossroads or provide a powerful insight. When we declare our intentions and consciously direct our energy positively, we are likely to make such choices, which can transform our lives.

Choices that invite miracles are initiated by cocreation. In cocreation, light energy gives power to pure thought and then energizes our thinking process so we can experience incidents of divine synchronicity, which we might call "co-incidents." We can learn from such divine synchronicities when we remain consciously aware enough to respond instead of reacting.

An example of such co-incidents is a series of experiences my client Joanne, a tenured teacher, had after deciding to move from Cleveland to Chicago. First, she declared her intention to relocate to another city, find a new inspiring job, and meet the woman of her dreams. A few days later, while sitting at her desk contemplating moving, she received a phone call from an old friend inviting her to come stay with her in Chicago the following weekend. Immediately, Joanne felt her heart blast open, a ringing in her ears, and a surge of energy moving up and down her spine, as if to affirm the "rightness" of this invitation to a woman who was more inclined to plan her trips far in advance. Aware that her logical brain had given way to pure conscious awareness, Joanne decided to follow her heart and go to Chicago.

While in Chicago, Joanne found the city exciting and met many people who worked in her own arena of higher education, so she decided to relocate at the end of her school year even though she had neither working nor living accommodations lined up there. No sooner did she make this decision than she received an offer to interview with a nonprofit educational agency for a consulting position, which she immediately accepted. Despite the hardship of giving up her teaching position and separating from her family and friends, she made the move, knowing that she was being led by spirit across any obstacles that stood between her and her dreams.

Six months later, Joanne came to see me, eager to fill me in on her new life. By this time she had found a lovely apartment in Chicago and been given the consulting position, which took her to Washington, DC on a regular basis. During her most recent trip there, she had met a woman she strongly connected with, who shared her core values and desire for spiritual growth. The longer we talked, the more she suspected this woman might be the beloved partner she had summoned into her life.

In such moments we may become disoriented, physically tense, or even paralyzed as we suddenly realize that our thoughts or actions have resulted in a mysterious convergence of energies. We may feel like a computer crashing when we try to access too many files at the same time, causing some to be erased from the hard drive. But if we trust our expanded conscious awareness and then pay attention to the physical, emotional, and spiritual signs that guide us, we can pause, breathe, and open our hearts to clear any confusion so we can respond rather than react.

A series of choices that inspired a miracle for me several years ago was when I had a routine mammogram and the results revealed calcifications in my right breast that could be an indication of breast cancer. Since a needle biopsy was inconclusive, I decided to have a lumpectomy. As I sat in my doctor's office, a million thoughts went through my head at once, such as, "What if I lose my breast?" "What if I die?" and "Who will take care of my children?" The irony in this situation was that I had been considering getting a surgical breast reduction in the next year.

As difficult as this situation was for me, I knew that I was being given a wake-up call to open my heart, accept my female body, and release my deep-seated self-consciousness. I also recognized that the therapeutic work I did made me highly vulnerable to potential problems because of the emotional processing that can congest the heart center, an area of the body uniquely associated with giving and nurturing. Aware that my self-healing required action, I set a clear intention for wellness and called in what was to be my energetic support team: my massage therapist, David, friend and professional trans-channel, Bryan, and my beloved husband, Doug. David and I focused on releasing energy blocks, especially around my heart center. Bryan and I worked on energetically releasing fear-based patterns that had created the energy blocks and opening my heart to light energy for self-healing. Through our sacred covenant of partnership, Doug and I explored sensual play to release the self-consciousness that was blocking my energies. I also meditated every day using a Foundation in Light CD that opened me to higher levels of spiritual awareness so I could release energy blocks at the soul level. Finally, several weeks before the surgery I legally changed my last name, which was my maiden name, to my married name, a change that I believed would separate my personal and professional identities and validate my core being rather than my identity structure.

A week before the surgery I traveled with my husband and daughter to New York City to relax and have fun. Near the end of our trip, we visited the Metropolitan Museum of Art, where we went our separate ways. Doug and Alex went to explore the impressionist exhibit, and I was drawn to the sculpture exhibit, with its view of Central Park. While sitting quietly on a bench in the garden, I immediately felt a sense of disorientation as my vision became blurred, causing me to see everything through a haze. As I opened my heart to this experience, I sensed a shift in my entire being, affirming my connection to a divine source and presenting the insight that everything was going to be okay.

I eventually rejoined my husband and daughter, and we left the museum to walk in Central Park. While there, I continued to experience this conscious awareness and felt as if everything before this moment had disintegrated. In my trancelike state, I reached in my pocket, feeling for my new leather gloves that I had received from my husband and realized I had lost one. My husband traced my path back to the bench in the sculpture exhibit but never found my glove, whereupon I had an intuitive feeling that it had disappeared along with the possibility of breast cancer. At this point, we left the park and took a taxi to the hotel.

The day after we returned home from New York City I had the lumpectomy, and the following week the results from the biopsy were negative for breast cancer. Because these results were unexpected, my surgeon requested that the needle biopsy sample be reanalyzed and subsequently told me I had cancer after all. In complete disbelief and feeling like I had been jerked backwards into a past reality, I was led down the hall by the nurse to schedule radiation and chemotherapy treatments.

A few hours later, when I was able to step outside of the situation and see it in a different light, I realized that my doctor was doing his job but was not my partner in wellness. Later that day, I called and thanked him for his assistance, took his recommendation under advisement, and gave myself permission to follow my heart. Trusting myself implicitly, I decided to hold off on the radiation and chemotherapy and continued to pursue my personal path of wellness.

Over the next year, I continued working with my energetic support team, monitored my body, and invited a medical partner into my healing process. This decision made friends and family panic and even question my sanity. I was surprised by how some of them tried to convince me to follow the traditional medical path, but their views allowed me to compassionately see how afraid people can become when they think they are about to lose someone they love. Although my husband was anxious and didn't necessarily hold my point of view, he was a true partner, supporting my choices throughout this time. For him, this was especially hard as it brought up the pain of losing his first wife to a sudden heart attack and his mother to a terminal illness over the previous seven years.

A year later, I found a breast surgeon who honored my choices even though she did not necessarily agree with them and became a true partner in my healing process. I followed through on her recommendations for a follow-up MRI, ultrasound, and mammogram. The results of these tests again were negative, validating the choices I had made in absolute trust of myself and inspiring what I consider a miracle.

In situations that challenge us, we have to let go and trust ourselves to make discerning choices. We also have to follow our hearts, even if it means going against people we love or authority figures. Being able to access conscious awareness gives us the confidence to make these choices that invite miracles as we cocreate our reality.

## Building an Energetic Support Team

As we develop a soul-hearted relationship with ourselves, we invite into our lives people who love us unconditionally, without judging, enabling, or interfering with our choices and actions, to form our energetic support team. Such an energetic support team will ultimately consist of kindred spirits who encourage the full expression of our true being rather than our ego-driven identity or the roles we play to survive in the world. As such, they will motivate us to continue releasing patterns, accessing our true being, and cocreating our reality for a more fulfilling future.

While selecting members of our energetic support team, we are likely to realize that people with whom we have had the longest or closest relationships, including some family members or friends, might not qualify as team members. Using conscious awareness, we may notice that they are actually invested in having us *retain* our fear-based patterns and limited choices. For instance, our transformations may trigger resistance or defensiveness within them. Our changes may especially challenge those who are afraid to see they are not living up to their own potential. Thus, although our clarity can help catalyze everyone in relationship with us to confront their own patterns, some may disconnect from us and even project their feelings of fear or pain onto us, or blame us for the unraveling of their lives. People with whom we in turn are inclined to suppress our needs or dismiss our desires are not candidates for our energetic support team.

In my own experience, I have found that an energetic support team is often revealed when we are moving through a transition or dealing with a difficult situation—times when others tend to show their true character. An example of one such situation occurred while my brother, Matt, and friend and mentor, Bryan, supported me when I needed to refinance my mortgage, change the title to my house, and generate more income to complete a divorce. As my energetic support team, they helped me trust myself despite my worries that the loan would not go through because I was single, self-employed, and had few assets. After the loan was approved, I realized that the combination of Matt's and Bryan's energies with my own had created a clear intention that had manifested.

Building an energetic support team requires careful evaluation of people we know to decide which ones will unconditionally endorse our choices for a more fulfilling future. The following are suggested guidelines to use in selecting candidates for an energetic support team.

First, observe your relationships to identify individuals who can serve the most supportive functions. Many support systems are set up to perpetuate the patterns of struggle, failure, victimization, or even illness. Instead, select healthy support systems comprised, for example, of such people as psychotherapists, spiritual guides, or soul-connected friends who can encourage your personal transformation.

Second, be sure your intentions are positive so that the people you gather around you will assist in sustaining your well-being. Then work on maintaining your energetic support team by periodically adding or eliminating members in keeping with your soul progression.

An example of using this evaluation method to build an energetic support team is my client Kathleen who, at age thirty-four, came to me seeking to change her life and engage in a healthy romantic relationship. The first step I asked her to take was to establish a loving and trusted relationship with herself before entering into an unconditionally loving relationship with someone else. Because of my guidance, she saw me as a member of her energetic support team.

With my assistance, Kathleen began assessing her current relationships to identify other members of her energetic support team. This was not an easy undertaking as it activated within her strong waves of separation anxiety. She had to move past her fear of being alone by trusting that she could foster healthy, supportive relationships in the future.

As our work continued, she began to let go of her unhealthy relationships and invited new people into her life who supported her unconditionally and eventually comprised her energetic support team. Without judgment or personal investment in her choices, her energetic support team inspired her to express herself creatively and encouraged her to follow her heart to manifest the life she envisioned.

As a result, Kathleen subsequently discovered that fully realizing herself depended not on being in a romantic relationship but on her acceptance and love of herself and making the best use of this energetic support system. Whenever people asked her if she was in a relationship, she would answer, "I am in a loving, committed relationship with myself and everyone who supports me."

To manifest our dreams, it is important to let go of our expectations of being supported in any way that is conditional, even by family and friends, and to establish an energetic support team that guides us unconditionally. As we continually evaluate our relationships to refine this team, we have to remain aware of our true being and surround ourselves with others who help us manifest our hearts' desires. As Henry David Thoreau said: "Go confidently in the direction of your dreams. Live the life you've imagined."[2]

The ability to cocreate our reality in every moment is a divine gift as well as our personal responsibility. All it takes to spark this cocreation is one pearl of light, the seed of possibility. With that we can become a conduit for channeling energy to manifest our dreams from an array of infinite possibilities. Answering this call to cocreation while taking full responsibility for our life circumstances, is what it means to be in soul-hearted partnership with ourselves.

## Practicing the Principles in Chapter Five

1. *Practice declaring intentions clearly then making conscious choices to manifest them.* Select a word or phrase that represents a positive intention for the day, month, or year. Write each intention on a Post-it Note, and place them wherever you will be able notice them, or write them in your journal. Then each time you see an intention, breathe in and affirm it.

2. *Practice accepting responsibility for cocreating your reality.* Hold yourself accountable for every choice you make, and actively make new choices to change your life. Handle things that happen with assuredness and ease so you stay aligned with your intent. To ensure that your choices will serve you well, pause before making each one and ask: "Am I making the best choice with the information I have right now?" and "Is this the best use of my time and energy?"

3. *Practice being response-able in different situations.* Use conscious awareness to respond instead of react to circumstances. Bless anyone who cuts in front of you in traffic or in a check-out lane, quickly forgive others' unkind remarks or unresolved grievances, and respect their points of view.

4. *Practice making discerning choices based on the guidance of spirit.* Influence the quality of your choices by listening to the voice of spirit through your heart rather than by focusing on a specific outcome. As new information comes your way, check with your heart to see if it resonates with you. If it does, use the information to screen and eliminate choices that are not appropriate to your being at this time, and to make more suitable choices. The more discerning your choices are, the more you will experience physical, mental, and spiritual well-being.

5. *Build an energetic support team.* Evaluate your relationships to see who qualifies to be on your energetic support team. Also invite onto your team trusted others who interact with you in an unconditionally loving way. The primary job of this team is to energetically support your intentions and fullest soul potential.

# Chapter Six

## SUSTAINING SOUL-HEARTED PARTNERSHIP
## WITH OURSELVES

"People say that what we're all seeking is a meaning for life.
I think that what we're really seeking is an experience of being alive,
so that our life experiences on the purely physical plane
will have resonance within our innermost being and reality,
so that we can actually feel the rapture of being alive."

—JOSEPH CAMPBELL

USTAINING A SOUL-HEARTED PARTNERSHIP with ourselves is the ground-work for the shared experience of soul-hearted partnership. This means maintaining trust in our connection with source, listening to the voice of spirit through our hearts, releasing negative patterns, and manifesting intentions for a more fulfilling personal life. It requires continually letting go of the life we have chosen until now so we can cocreate the life we want to share with a partner in the future. Using conscious awareness, we can witness how spirit guides us to opportunities and choices that result in a life based less on fear and insecurity, and more on spiritual transformation. But it is equally important to realize that sustaining soul-hearted partnership with ourselves necessitates constant personal evolution.

*Beyond the Proverbial Pink Bubble*
Personal growth and spiritual transformation is not a goal that can be attained but an ongoing process. We are often seduced into thinking that once we have experienced personal growth and a spiritual breakthrough we no longer need to focus on change. We then allow our momentary feeling of gratification to become a pink bubble enveloping us in feelings of security and triumph. Like Glenda, the good witch of the north in *The Wizard of Oz*, we remain inside this bubble of illusion, ignoring the guidance of spirit

through our hearts telling us we still have a journey of transformation ahead. But remaining inside this pink bubble and resisting change creates conditions in which old patterns can surface and arrest further personal transformation, threatening the foundation for either sustaining our soul-hearted relationship with ourselves or building one with another person. To move forward, we have to burst the pink bubble and sustain our true being.

The following story exemplifies what happens when a person stays trapped in their pink bubble. As Beth focused on fulfilling her own dreams after a divorce, she decided to leave the accounting practice she had shared with her ex-husband and open her own practice at home, a risky undertaking now that she was a single mother with children to support. Gradually, she manifested her intention of being the sole proprietor of her own business and congratulated herself on her new independence and spiritual transformation. But the pink bubble she was in obscured her perspective so that she failed to recognize she still had more inner work to do.

At this point, her old patterns surfaced, particularly her pattern of being a caretaker. Having let go of her marriage, she soon found life unbearable since she had no one to take care of other than her children. This made her feel anxious because she had always equated taking care of someone with feeling needed and important.

After I suggested that she temporarily refrain from dating to eliminate the distraction of initiating a new relationship, she agreed to take time to heal and work on her relationship with herself. But she convinced herself that a month was all she needed, after which she initiated a new transitional relationship, which was destined to fail because she had not yet uncovered and healed the source of her pain. Succumbing to her insecurities, she looked again for stability outside herself and focused not on manifesting her dreams but on supporting her boyfriend's schemes. For example, instead of setting aside money for herself and her children she used her savings to pay for their vacations.

Finally taking a good look at herself and her new relationship Beth realized she had reverted to a more subtle version of her old role as caretaker in a relationship with someone who played the role of victim, letting her partner's desires consume her own.

Often in relationships, because we so desperately want a fairy tale romance, we block our access to spiritual information and make excuses for relationship deficits. Trying to make the relationship work at all costs, we ignore the surfacing of patterns. Needy and afraid to be alone, we begin doubting our ability to generate opportunities through intention, and we ask ourselves: "What if this is the last chance for me to be in a relationship?" "If I leave the relationship, will I end up alone?" and "Can I earn a living and take care of myself on my own?" Such behavior leads to stagnation in the same kinds of situations we have experienced in the past.

For these reasons, we have to take time to be alone and discover how to sustain a soul-hearted partnership with ourselves before entering into a new relationship with another person. The time spent alone gives us the chance to notice cues alerting us to patterns that are resurfacing, so we can release them before they lure us into the next unhealthy relationship.

In short, evaluating the situation in a safe space allows us to better understand our own needs and desires and avoid repeating negative patterns in a new relationship. This can prevent a later agonizing realization that we are not only repeating an unhealthy history but are enveloped by a pink bubble that will inhibit further spiritual transformation.


## Relationship Life Cycles

Like the life cycles we move through as the years unfold, relationships also have life cycles—some lasting for only a brief period and others a season or a lifetime. To make suitable choices in relationships for particular periods in our lives, it is helpful to look at three major types of relationship that, together, can satisfy everything from need fulfillment to spiritual growth.

First, there is *transitional relationship*, based on momentary needs. This type of relationship includes casual encounters for the purpose of sex or friendship, healing, ego validation, overcoming loneliness, or dealing with a desire for control and security. During transitions, intense times of self-healing and personal discovery, we tend to initiate relationships with people who exhibit negative patterns to which we are attracted, or who are releasing such patterns themselves and are in a position to assist us in learning to love ourselves. We are drawn by the energy of these people, in transition themselves, as a way of stabilizing the unsettling period in our own lives. The mutual exchange of energy, while temporary, can be satisfying and supportive. As long as both individuals are aware of the purpose of their relationship, their needs are being met, and they are observing healthy boundaries and treating each other with respect, they can both benefit greatly from the experience.

The second type of relationship is *contractual relationship*, in which individuals come together to create something for a common purpose. The most customary form of contractual relationship involves childbearing, usually in a marriage. A contractual relationship can also exist for such purposes as establishing social status or developing a business enterprise.

Finally, there is true *soul-hearted partnership*, in which both individuals have a fully realized relationship with themselves as well as with each other. In such a relationship, partners can develop spiritually in concert with each other, and thus the relationship can last a lifetime without becoming unhealthy or unfulfilling. And because it is a partnership between two powerfully expressed beings for the purpose of soul progression, soul-hearted partnership can be seen as the ultimate form of spiritual relationship.

In addition to temporary or lifelong relationships, we also experience temporary or lifelong friendships. Many friendships are based on specific life cycles, personal interests, and activities. For example, we may have friends associated with school, business enterprises, activities like skiing or biking, attending movies or theater, shopping, or dinners and conversation. When friends have a deep emotional bond and a soul connection that transcends all life cycles, it can last a lifetime. These are the rare friends who know our strengths and weaknesses, are honest with us, love us unconditionally, and can thus reflect our true being. We may have a disagreement with them or not see them for long periods of time, but our soul connection is maintained, and they are vital to our soul progression. Such lifelong friendships make up our core energetic support team; these are our soul companions. In his book *Spiritual Relationships*, Paramhansa Yogananda sums up the essence of such friendships when he says, "Friendship is the universal spiritual attraction that unites souls in the bond of divine love."[1]

Our longing for love often convinces us that all relationships are meant to last forever and keeps us from distinguishing between the various types. In the movie *The Mirror Has Two Faces*, Barbra Streisand, who portrays a college professor, poignantly expresses our longing for love and passion in our lives: "We all want to fall in love. Why? Because it makes us feel completely alive, where every sense is heightened, every emotion is magnified. Our everyday reality is shattered and we are flung into the heavens. It may only last a moment, an hour, an afternoon, but that doesn't diminish its value because we are left with memories that we treasure for the rest of our lives."[2]

Knowing the life cycles of different types of relationships helps us adjust our expectations accordingly, ensuring that we actively maintain lifelong relationships and willingly let go of temporary ones. Many couples fall in love and marry blinded by physical attraction, which makes them feel alive. This form of transitional relationship usually originates when individuals are vulnerable and looking for an experience to either transform or ground them. But as the steam of lust and infatuation clears they see the relationship for what it is and become dissatisfied.

Much the same can be said of contractual relationships. Despite their shared mission and positive aspects, we must be aware that such relationships are not complete because they are usually not based on a genuine partnership in which each person is independently fulfilled. Therefore, it is essential to discern, through the use of conscious awareness, whether a relationship is based on the common core values of love, trust, integrity, intimacy, and a soul connection or is merely functioning in fulfillment of an agreement or as a temporary distraction or emotional crutch.

Contractual and transitional relationships can become soul-hearted partnerships when there is a mutual desire for spiritual growth and an adherence to its core values. But when there isn't, attempting to sustain these temporary relationships after they have fulfilled their purpose can cause suffering, especially those based on a short-term physical or emotional dependency. An example of such a scenario is when two strangers meet at a bar, become physically attracted, leave together, and a year later marry without any real basis for a lifetime commitment. What starts out as a short-term affair that fulfilled mutual sexual and companionship needs thus becomes a marriage of two incompatible people. Holding on to any relationship beyond its purpose prevents us from directing the flow of our energy to manifest a deeply committed, lifelong partnership.

Unfortunately, people who automatically think a relationship should last forever may fail to assess the purpose of their relationships and thus confuse transitional or contractual ones with the lifetime soul-hearted type. Some people even marry partners they know are incompatible, making a commitment to cherish the union until death do them part—a decision likely to be disastrous to both parties, especially when the relationship's purpose has been fulfilled early on and there is little spiritual basis for continuing the union. In such relationships, partners frequently feel trapped, which leads to inconsideration, bickering, boredom, and even depression. At this point, it is time for one or both partners to make the constructive decision to move on. Too often, however, instead of both partners acknowledging what has occurred and accepting responsibility, they individually experience anger, guilt, and resentment and engage in a battle leading to separation. Others continue battling for years because they share money, children, and social lives. In this worst case scenario, the partners lose all that was once valuable and meaningful about their relationship.

It is important to see transitional and contractual relationships for what they are: a means of coping with a difficult or transformative period in life with the help of another person who fulfills our needs, helps us grow, and adds joy to our circumstances. Such relationships, when entered into honestly and lovingly, can be beneficial if they propel both individuals along their chosen spiritual paths. Yet once their mission is fulfilled, it is usually time to let go and progress to another level of relationship, for which the transitional or contractual partner may not be appropriate. In such a case, we can honor the partner by expressing gratitude for their being, lovingly release the relationship, and move on. For our own well-being, it's important not to make transitional or contractual relationships lifelong ones or stay in such relationships beyond their spiritual purpose.

The following example traces the evolution and dissolution of a transitional relationship. When Marie, a twenty-seven-year-old freelance writer, first met Tom at a local bar, she became quickly infatuated with the idea that he could potentially be her lifelong partner. Each was in the midst of a tumultuous transition: Marie had just broken off a five-year relationship with her live-in boyfriend, and Tom had been recently divorced and had two children. Marie saw Tom as kind, and a loving, responsible father. For the first time, she felt nurtured in the way that she cared for others, and their passionate lovemaking exceeded any experience she had ever had with a lover. Their sexual attraction, however, mistakenly convinced her that they also shared a deep spiritual connection, and she fell head over heels for him without assessing, from a healthy detached point of view, the spiritual purpose of their relationship.

Looking at Tom initially through a lens of infatuation diminished her ability to see red flags, such as Tom's neediness and dependency on her to make him feel secure. For example, he would call her throughout the day and night, wanting to spend most of his time with her, and had few friends and interests outside of the relationship. Worse, she didn't always feel good about herself while with him since apart from their sexual attraction, they did not share core values or a desire for spiritual growth.

Subsequently, the fire of the relationship flickered for only ten months before being extinguished. Nevertheless, during that time the relationship did fulfill one of Marie's major needs—to regain confidence in her sexuality. And it had also helped her progress in her ability to recognize and release negative patterns evident in her previous relationships. This time it took her only ten months and minimal drama to recognize and release the pattern of avoidance and insecurity that had kept her stuck a lot longer in previous self-destructive relationships. But because she ignored the red flags, she stayed in her relationship with Tom longer than was necessary. If Marie had been able to earlier detect the physical, mental, and spiritual cues warning her that she was in a temporary relationship and not a lifetime partnership, she might have had a broader perspective on her situation.

In temporary relationships such as this, we often experience a struggle between our heads and our hearts that keeps us from listening to the voice of spirit. We close the eyes of the heart, succumbing to our fears of loss, rejection, and scarcity and diminishing our sense of ourselves for a momentary "fix" of physical attraction, emotional security, or personal calling, leading us to make pattern-driven, unenlightened choices.

To avoid settling for a relationship that inhibits spiritual growth, it is crucial to be aware that strong sexual attraction often characterizes the first stage of a new relationship based on infatuation. Physical attraction can, however, diminish our ability to observe the relationship from a healthy detached point of view. This is when we fall head over heels—or more often, "head over heart." As a result, we can become attached to a relationship physically or as an emotional crutch, and lose our common sense and our trust in ourselves to make informed decisions. Dismissing the guidance of the voice of spirit, we then become susceptible to repeating past patterns rather than spiritually progressing as individuals toward the future cocreation of a soul-hearted partnership.

## Interviewing Potential Partners

As we continue the inner spiritual work necessary to sustain our full self-expression, we may declare an intention to enter into an intimate relationship with another person. In preparation for such an event, we can use the spiritual principles we have practiced to assist us in interviewing potential partners so we can choose discerningly.

Many people spend more time and energy interviewing prospective plumbers, landscapers, and Internet companies than potential partners. They ask for references, talk with current customers, and check track records with the Better Business Bureau; yet, they do little if any research when choosing prospective partners. Because of lust, neediness, or fear of being alone, we allow impulse, infatuation, and patterns to influence these choices.

Instead, we can interview potential partners by using specific spiritual principles. First, we prepare by listening to the voice of spirit through our hearts, which will assist us in maintaining a healthy detached point of view and activating conscious awareness. Next, we observe various people we are considering dating, are currently dating, or are in relationship with and ask our hearts these questions: "Does this person demonstrate a fully expressed relationship with themselves, and is this evident in daily life?" "How do I feel about myself when I am with this person?" and "Do I see myself as being happier in this relationship?" Ideally a potential partner will be trustworthy, loving, playful, and exude a sheer love of life. When we are with such a person, we will feel inspired, safe, and free to express our true being. The individual will take responsibility for their own weaknesses, show integrity in the enlightened choices they make, do the inner spiritual work for personal transformation, and increasingly develop to their fullest soul potential. The following qualification mantra is helpful to use when interviewing potential partners: "Who you are, I must love. How you act and treat me, I have to like. And most of all, my loving heart has to be earned."

In other words, we begin preparing for the interview process by activating our conscious awareness. Ultimately, we manifest our true partner by knowing who we are and what we want in a loving relationship, then projecting the qualities we want to see in a partner.

Here is an example of how to use conscious awareness when interviewing a potential partner. Alex's personal transformation began when she came to me and entered into the spiritual training necessary to shift the quality of her relationships. Throughout her life, she had trudged through many dysfunctional relationships that usually ended with unnecessary drama, disappointment, and painful lessons. Her most recent relationship had left her feeling discouraged about how to even attract a true partner into her life.

Initially, I suggested to Alex that she stop seeking a partner and first develop a relationship with herself and her energetic support team. I proposed that she declare her intention to have healthy and loving relationships with people who would support her physically, emotionally, and spiritually in her life. I also recommended that she be willing to explore her behavioral patterns and her past relationships. As she began this self-discovery, she learned to trust and love herself, take more responsibility for her choices, and in time use the spiritual information she received through her heart to evaluate her choices. Most importantly, I helped her see that every future relationship would be a life-changing opportunity to practice recognizing and releasing patterns, live more fully expressed, and thus manifest a more fulfilling life.

Integrating these principles, Alex became a magnet for people who wanted to grow spiritually and experience their fullest expression. Many of these people either became a member of her energetic support team or simply desired a relationship with her. This led her to evaluate her relationships on a continuous basis.

After spending time becoming a loving partner to herself, she made a clear intention to manifest a relationship with an intimate partner. With her energetic support team available for feedback, she consciously invited in potential partners to help her fine-tune her vision of an intimate relationship. And while interviewing potential partners as she dated, she gained insight about the qualities she wanted in a partner.

Spiritual information she received through her heart guided her to have fun without becoming infatuated and emotionally attached too quickly. Engaging her conscious awareness, she recognized and released her patterns and any relationships that were not appropriate to her true being at this time in her life. Eliminating unhealthy relationships further inspired her to create healthier ones. She knew she could not settle for anything less than a relationship with a trustworthy and beloved partner.

One element that was important for her in manifesting a future partnership was the idea of sharing travel. Intending to share her love of travel with someone, Alex purchased a beautiful set of designer luggage that she would use first to travel alone and then with her future partner.

Before Alex met her future partner Nick, she dated four other men. While interviewing each of these "applicants," she accessed her conscious awareness through her heart as she observed their words, actions, and choices. What she witnessed gave her clarity about whether to continue or stop dating each of these individuals.

With my guidance, Alex saw that the first potential partners she interviewed were actually subtler versions of men with whom she had had prior relationships. She wondered why she continued to attract men who exhibited the same patterns. As she examined her previous relationships and listened to the voice of her heart, she became aware of her tendency to attract men who were in transition and usually self-destructive and self-absorbed. Ultimately she recognized that she was summoning such men to her because of her own patterns of rescue, obligation, and avoidance.

Alex soon concluded that none of the men she was currently dating was a match for her, as they were merely variations of her previous partners. This affirmed for her that she was looking for someone who was sustaining a fully realized relationship with themselves and willing to enter into the shared experience of soul-hearted partnership. As a result, she realized that she was better off at this time choosing to be alone than living a mere fantasy of the relationship she desired.

A year later, Alex had advanced from declaring her intention of soul-hearted partnership to manifesting the possibility of it in her life. By then she saw that in refusing to settle for unhealthy relationships and being happy alone she had opened a flow of energy that supported her intention. She realized it was up to her to direct this energy positively by making discerning choices that would lead her to the relationship she wanted.

One day while leaving a neighborhood coffeehouse, Alex caught Nick's eye when he held the door open for her. As she walked out, she followed her intuition to look back. While standing in the doorway, Nick was looking at her. They gazed at each other, smiling, held in suspended animation. As a surge of pure energy moved through each of their hearts, they knew this synchronistic moment was opening the possibility of a relationship that would transform their lives.

Eventually, Nick invited Alex back inside to join him for coffee. Alex, her heart open, trusted herself and accepted his invitation. She sensed that at that moment she had let go of her past, along with her expectations of the future. Through her conscious awareness, she experienced this as a moment of cocreation, of the possibility of scripting her own fairy tale.

Alex had attracted Nick into her life as a potential partner who shared her intention for spiritual growth and aligned with her in the love of travel. As they began building a relationship, Alex made sure to maintain a loving, supportive relationship with herself and watched to see that Nick did as well. Subsequently, after dating a few months, they took a trip to Belize using the luggage Alex had chosen for this purpose.

In contrast, when we fail to use our conscious awareness to assess potential partners, we are apt to make unenlightened choices that reflect the reemergence of past patterns, as the following scenario illustrates. You notice that the person you are currently dating is staying out late several nights a week and drinking excessively—self-destructive behaviors this individual's friends seem to support. When you express your concern, the individual quickly becomes defensive and minimizes, but does not eliminate, the late-night pursuits. Moreover, this person constantly talks about changing their lifestyle and career and putting their finances in order but never follows through with such plans. Instead, you see that the individual refuses to take responsibility for past mistakes and lacks positive intentions for the future.

As these red flags emerge within the relationship, you dismiss them, avoid confrontation with the individual, and even make excuses or alibis for their self-destructive behavior. You ignore the voice of spirit urging you to see that you have assumed the role of caretaker focused on rescuing this person and fixing their problems. Instead of developing a potential partnership, you find that you have produced a facsimile of your past relationships.

The person's resistance to taking responsibility for existing patterns and refusal to receive supportive feedback or examine thoughts, feelings, and choices underlying the destructive behavior indicates that this individual is not in a healthy relationship with themselves, let alone you. Once you acknowledge what is happening, you wonder how you ended up in a recycled version of past relationships.

To avoid such a discouraging scenario, we need to use our conscious awareness to interview potential partners. Then we can ask ourselves, without self-judgment or recrimination, "How can I avoid re-creating my usual scenario of relationship?" Our honest answer, coming through our hearts, will guide us in making choices appropriate to our true being.

We also must make certain not to ignore any spiritual information we are receiving through our heart telling us that an individual is not a potential partner. The following story is a good example of what can happen when we ignore such information. Jordan had started interviewing potential partners through an online dating service. As she read their inquiries to her profile, she used conscious awareness, searching for men who shared common core values. One man caught her attention, and she decided to meet him at a local restaurant.

Instead of pausing and centering herself before walking into the restaurant, Jordan rushed there from work, overwhelmed with anticipation. As she introduced herself, she felt her throat constrict, her chest tighten, and immediately sensed a lack of self-confidence. When he ordered a drink for her without asking her whether she wanted one, Jordan felt her stomach flip-flop. From what seemed like a distance, she heard herself tell the waitress that she didn't want the drink he had ordered, but she couldn't get the words out of her mouth.

Throughout the evening his pattern of dominance and control continued to surface, making Jordan increasingly uncomfortable. The information coming through her heart had already clearly indicated that continuing the date wasn't in her best interest, but the resurgence of an old pattern of seeking approval blocked out the information so that she acquiesced to everything her date suggested. After a few hours, her date decided it was time to leave, put his arm around her shoulder, and seductively guided her to his car. Feeling as if she were in a drug-induced stupor, she got into his car and found herself fighting off his sexual advances. Finally jolted from her altered state, she recognized this red flag, told him to stop, and got out of the car.

As I helped her evaluate the situation in hindsight, Jordan realized that she had fallen into her old pattern of seeking approval, especially from men, and not trusting what she sensed. She traced the source of the pattern to her relationship with her father, which was based on conditional love. To gain his love and approval, she had always tried to be a "good girl," doing things that attracted his attention and made her feel accepted. As she examined her past relationships, she recognized that she had deferred to others to validate that she was lovable—behavior she had repeated with her recent date. Although she had received information through her heart warning her of his unsuitability as a potential partner, her pattern of seeking approval had caused her to ignore it until the situation had become desperate.

As a result of this experience, Jordan knew that it was time for her to learn to love herself unconditionally so she would stop seeking approval from others to validate her. Doing so increased her confidence, empowered her to listen to information through her heart about her dates, and leave any situation that wasn't consistent with her choice to live in soul-hearted partnership with herself. D. H. Lawrence writes, "Those that go searching for love only make manifest their own lovelessness, and the loveless never find love, only the loving find love, and they never have to seek it."[3]

Many of us evade breakups because we erroneously expect the other person to outgrow their patterns. But in reality, while assessing a relationship it is important to realize that if we do not see the other person functioning well right now, chances are we will not later. To become more aware of when to end an unhealthy relationship, ask yourself: "Does this person see and express the truth about their weaknesses and patterns, and is it supported by a desire to change them?" "Do I observe this person taking full responsibility for thoughts, feelings, and choices in life?" and "Is this person willing to do the inner spiritual work it takes to cocreate a soul-hearted relationship?"

Finally, when using conscious awareness to interview potential partners, keep the following analogy in mind as guidance. Imagine you are a lamp. As such, it is your responsibility to make sure you are correctly wired with no short circuits, have good bulbs, an exquisite shade, and functional hardware. You make sure you are the best lamp you can be and know how to turn yourself on. One day you notice another lamp that attracts you. So you examine it to be sure it has no major tears, broken cords, or anything you will have to fix. It may have a different shade, unusual hardware, or even a loose switch that can easily be tightened, but you ensure that everything essential works and that the lamp stays lit on a continuous basis.

The light of our being attracts potential partners. But it is up to us to maintain our own energy source and to interview potential partners to ascertain whether they are appropriate for us at this time in our lives.

## Soul Mates and Soul-Hearted Partners

Soul mates appear in life for reasons that often have to do with the soul's purpose on earth and our spiritual progression. They enhance our lives by providing insights, unconditional love, and assistance with challenges. They often appear serendipitously in sync with us, arriving as if in response to some spiritual law of attraction. When the reason for which they have been summoned is resolved, they are free to stay or move on. If one should remain in your life as a soul-hearted partner, it is a blessing for which to be grateful.

Many people assume that there is only one true soul mate for each person and that we have to persistently seek out this person to be happy. In reality, however, there may be many with whom we can interact throughout a lifetime. The relentless search for the one perfect person to complete us is one of the ego's most persuasive delusions. Your spirit does not have a vested interest in any one person; indeed, there are many individuals on earth who are here to guide your soul's journey and help you see your life from a more cosmic perspective.

Recognizing a soul mate is not difficult. We often see a special look in their eyes and experience an inner knowing of soul connection. When encountering such a person, we might sense a surge of electric current move through our body, feel physically at ease in their presence, and realize that they have struck a deep chord within our hearts. We may even feel as if we have known this person for ages without having ever met them before. This sense of familiarity and accord with a soul mate is expressed by the poet Mevlana Jalaluddin Rumi in his book *Music Master:* "The minute I heard my first love story, I started looking for you, not knowing how blind that was. Lovers don't finally meet somewhere. They're in each other all along."[4]

With soul mates, time and distance seem meaningless. Even if we see such a person only once a year, when you encounter them again it is as if you have never been apart. It is a present-oriented experience with no future expectations. Also, soul mates have a pure energetic connection that does not have to be expressed within the physical parameters of a relationship. With such people you feel a common connection to a divine source. As Yogananda writes in *Spiritual Relationships*, "True friendship unites two souls so completely that they reflect the unity of spirit and its divine qualities."[5]

A soul-hearted partner is a soul mate with whom we develop and sustain intimacy not just at the soul level but on all levels—physical, mental, emotional, and spiritual. Whereas a soul mate is like a diamond in the rough, with its sparkle of potential, a soul-hearted partner is like a diamond that has been cut and polished to bring out its brilliance and put into a four-pronged setting of self-expression, unconditional love, intimacy, and absolute trust. Soul mates can become soul-hearted partners with whom we share our lives, but to live as soul mates, with a heart and soul connection, both partners have to arrest behavioral patterns, love unconditionally, trust unequivocally, and as much as possible, relate to each other being-to-being.

Manifesting soul-hearted partnership depends on our ability to completely love, accept, express ourselves without reservation, and trust our connection to source. Upon realizing these capabilities, it is in declaring our intention that we invite in soul-hearted partnership.


### Inviting In a Beloved Partner

Our personal experience of soul-hearted partnership, our trusted connection to source, and our energetic support team form the basis upon which we invite into our lives a beloved partner. According to spiritual principles, to attract a soul-hearted partnership into our lives, we need to first embody the characteristics we seek. For instance, if we want genuine love, we must be a loving person. If we desire absolute trust, we must be trustworthy. If we want true intimacy, we must be open and truthful with ourselves and others. In Rumi's words, "To find the beloved, you must become the beloved."[6]

The next step in attracting a beloved partner is to declare an intention for a partnership supported by our divine energy source. Trusting that our intention is being supported in this way, we invite into our lives a beloved partner. This process is facilitated by the fact that the beloved partner has declared an intention to have such a partnership energetically aligned with our intention.

Finally, to invite in a beloved partner, we must be out in front of our intention behaving as if this person already existed. One way to do this is by acting as if our beloved partner lives with us, by setting an extra place at the dinner table, sitting next to an unoccupied chair at the coffee shop, or keeping an extra pillow on the bed—thereby creating an energetic space for our partner to come into our lives. Because manifestation of intention is aided by visualization, it helps to imagine how we want our partner to interact with us. Another way to behave as if our beloved partner already existed is by aligning ourselves with the energetic vibration of love and light, and thus attracting people who also have a higher vibration and thus are most compatible with us. In addition, following our hearts and choosing well from among the people we have attracted into our lives will lead to a soul-hearted partnership in keeping with divine synchronicity.

The following story of David and Emma illustrates one way to cocreate reality through aligning energies and making a series of discerning choices that support the intention to attract a beloved partner into one's life. When the possibility emerged for developing a relationship with David, Emma was living her life happily as a single woman with three children and was not actively looking for a partner to complete her. She had already established a loving, trusted relationship with herself and her energetic support team while living through a difficult time of transition, characterized by self-healing and releasing her past relationships. She did, however, desire an intimate partner with whom she could share an even richer experience of life.

One spring afternoon, Emma took time to herself, strolling around her favorite lake and speaking her intention to the universe, saying, "I want a fully realized, loving partner with whom I can share my life." Her heart's desire was to have a partner who acknowledged her being, who did not need her to complete him, and who expressed his own personal power. As it turned out, her declaration opened an energetic portal to infinite possibilities, through which she had to move to manifest her intention.

Several days later, Emma encountered David at the party of a mutual friend. Although they had known each other for nearly two decades, having worked for the same financial institution, Emma had not seen him for many years. David, too, was going through an intense transitional period, having been recently divorced and not actively seeking a new partner. At this meeting, a spark ignited a heart-and-soul connection between them. Emma felt this moment of cocreation as if it were happening in slow motion outside the realm of logic. Opening her heart and following her intuition, Emma asked David to dance. At that moment, she began making a series of choices that were consistent with her intention of initiating a new relationship. She gently took David's hand and guided him to the dance floor. Responding to her request, David shyly shared that he rarely danced but felt drawn to dance with her then. Sensing that he could be her true partner, Emma invited David to accompany her home.

Expanding their conscious awareness opened David and Emma to being in tune with the events of divine synchronicity that had brought them together. Listening to the guidance of spirit, they followed the cues offered to them and made a myriad of choices that led them to a relationship.

When we invite in a beloved partner, we engage in the ultimate dance of soul-hearted partnership, sharing the joy, passion, and exuberance of our life with this person. The unending flow of positive energy that we exude affects how we wake up in the morning, walk and carry ourselves, handle disappointment, give and receive love, and sustain the partnership.

**The following poem, "Love after Love" by Derek Walcott, captures the essence of the personal experience of soul-hearted partnership:**

The time will come
when, with elation,
you will greet yourself arriving
at your own door, in your own mirror,
and each will smile at the other's welcome,

and say, sit here. Eat.
You will love again the stranger who was your self.
Give wine. Give bread. Give back your heart
to itself, to the stranger who has loved you

all your life, whom you ignored
for another, who knows you by heart.
Take down the love letters from the bookshelf,

the photographs, the desperate notes,
peel your own image from the mirror.
Sit. Feast on your life.[7]

PRACTICING THE PRINCIPLES IN CHAPTER SIX

1. *Assess whether you are living in a pink bubble that keeps you from continuous personal transformation.* Looking at your recent past, determine if the illusion of having triumphed over past patterns is preventing you from releasing them and doing more spiritual work. Then affirm to yourself that this pink bubble undermines your ongoing engagement in personal transformation.

2. *Practice taking purposeful breaks to gain perspective and thus avoid initiating a relationship from impulse.* Spend time alone to discover your vulnerabilities and release your insecurities. Ask yourself, "Am I initiating a relationship from a fear of being alone or for reasons of security, money, or status?" Check in with yourself when you feel ungrounded, excusing yourself from interactions and finding a place where you can center yourself, listen to the voice of spirit, and make choices consistent with this information.

3. *Evaluate your current relationships to see if they are appropriate to your current life cycle.* Since every relationship in which you participate is a barometer of how you see yourself, look at all your relationships and ask yourself: "What kind of relationships do I have, and are they appropriate to my current spiritual development and the life I desire?" "How do I feel about myself while in these relationships?" "Do I feel pulled back into patterns that are detrimental to my well-being?" and "What patterns and issues am I trying to resolve by being in certain relationships?"

4. *Interview potential partners with whom you are currently in relationship.* Listen to your heart and ask yourself: "Does this person express their true being, and is this supported by their choices?" "Do I see this person taking full responsibility for thoughts, feelings, and choices in life?" "Is this individual open to supportive feedback and new information?"

5. *Identify your soul mates and their special characteristics.* Pick out the soul mates in your life and the qualities you associate with them. Then reflect on the characteristics you would also like to have in a soul-hearted partner. List the qualities you would like to see in a partner, and strive to embody them.

6. *Envision your beloved partner.* Open your heart and visualize your beloved partner. To reinforce your image, share it with your energetic support team or write about it, refining the vision as you gain more information.

*7. Invite into your life a soul-hearted partner by acting as if this has already occurred.* Create a space for a beloved partner to come into your life by setting an extra place at dinner, sitting next to an unoccupied seat at the coffee shop, or keeping an extra pillow on your bed.

PART II

# The Shared Experience
# of Soul-Hearted Partnership

# Chapter Seven

## MASTERING THE SPIRITUAL PRINCIPLES
## OF SOUL-HEARTED PARTNERSHIP

"Love does not consist in gazing at each other
but in looking outward in the same direction."
—ANTOINE DE SAINT-EXUPÉRY

*T*HE GROUNDWORK FOR THE SHARED EXPERIENCE of soul-hearted partnership is established when two individuals accomplished in partner-
ing with themselves master the spiritual principles of partnership with
another. As in dance, we must first learn the basic steps and then practice
the techniques, embracing our mistakes as opportunities to develop more
inspired moves. Eventually we trust ourselves enough to stop looking at our
feet and gaze lovingly into our partner's eyes as we move through life in
graceful coordination with this person.

While further cultivating the relationship, we consistently recognize and
release energy blocks and patterns so that our evolving partnership becomes
more synchronized. Communicating soul to soul with our partner, we intu-
itively anticipate the next move without interrupting the flow of energy
between us.

### Relationships As Opportunities for Self-Realization

Relationships provide us with numerous opportunities for self-realization
by inspiring us to expand our conscious awareness, address our weaknesses,
and spiritually progress beyond what we can achieve alone. As such, they
invite us to realize a deeper sense of our true being. But because intimate
relationships are often challenging, many people believe they are better off
alone, unaware that such isolation will likely limit their capacity to experience genuine love, personal vulnerability, and intimacy. Moreover, relationships offer us valuable opportunities to examine ourselves in different ways,

get feedback about our patterns, attitudes, and imperfections that inhibit personal transformation, and increase our emotional and spiritual awareness. In the mirror of relationships, we can clearly observe the situations that cause our patterns to surface and also gain information to assist us in making better choices for a healthier and happier future. As Shakti Gawain, author of *Creative Visualization*, states: "The people we are in relationships with are always a mirror, reflecting our own beliefs. A relationship with another human being is one of the most powerful tools for growth that we have; if we look honestly at our relationships, we can see so much about how we have created them."[1]

Every relationship we create is purposeful and can offer us significant insights, even if it is only the insight that the relationship is unhealthy. Such useful information is available to us through every relationship no matter how important or insignificant, from a brief encounter with a store clerk to intimacy with a partner. All information from any of our relationships helps us interact with others and contributes to our overall spiritual growth. In effect, our purpose in every relationship is to love the person, accept the message, and apply whatever information we acquire to transform ourselves. As spiritual beings, we want to experience everything necessary to foster such transformation.

To comprehend how we acquire this beneficial information through relationships, we can practice observing ourselves interacting with another person, paying attention to the information we receive about ourselves in the form of physical sensations, thoughts, and feelings. For example, we can notice whether the feelings coming through us are love or fear, acceptance or judgment, or openheartedness or aversion. Then we can assess this information by asking ourselves the following questions: "Am I loving and sensitive toward this person, acknowledging the individual through eye contact or an engaging smile, or irritable or dismissive, ignoring the person and rushing to get to my next task?" "Do I treat others with utmost care and kindness, or am I self-absorbed and judgmental?" The answers to such questions will tell us how much we value the person and how respectful we are of others in general. For both practical and spiritual purposes, it is beneficial to treat all people with respect since maintaining positive interactions provides the best opportunity to cocreate positive outcomes in life. Because of the spiritual law of karma, it is crucial that we treat people with respect and kindness because whatever energy we send out into the universe will be sent back to us.

An example of such a positive encounter occurred when a friend and I met a sweet, young woman in an ice cream parlor. As we were playfully tasting the delicious flavors of gelato, the woman mentioned that the blackberry flavor was a great choice. When we started conversing with her and invited her and her husband to join us, they immediately told us they were separated. We explained that we had given a workshop that very afternoon on soul-hearted partnerships and, with their encouragement, offered our points of view on the subject. We ended by acknowledging that this co-incident was a matter of divine timing, and the couple agreed, remarking that they had gleaned more valuable information during our encounter than in several months of marital counseling. I immediately flashed onto a passage in *Course in Miracles* that points out: "When you meet anyone, remember it is a holy encounter. As you see him you will see yourself. As you treat him you will treat yourself. As you think of him you think of yourself. Never forget this, for in him you will find yourself or lose yourself."[2]

While even casual relationships can provide useful information for our spiritual growth, intimate relationships offer the most transformative information because they support a deeper exploration of patterns and imperfections. In such relationships, there are daily opportunities to not only gain insights into our patterns but also release negative reactions.

For example, suppose you struggle with a pattern of getting frustrated when things change or are out of your control. You notice that something you keep in a certain place has been moved and react irritably. In an intimate partnership you can learn to instead use such an opportunity to recognize and release your pattern, and respond rather than react, if only to maintain harmony within the relationship. Everything irritating us about others, psychologist Carl Jung advises, can lead us to understand ourselves. Even at the first sign of conflict within the relationship, you can be almost certain an underlying pattern belonging to either you or your partner has been triggered. Releasing it will unblock energy and shift your focus in the relationship. For instance, in this scenario you may realize that in the context of a loving, fulfilling relationship it really doesn't matter where the corkscrew has been placed.

Although the information we glean from the mirror of relationship is valuable, it only reflects the mindsets and patterns stored in the brain and not the core being. Like Alice in Wonderland as she steps through the looking glass, we can acquire information about our core being by looking through the window of expanded conscious awareness in our hearts. In essence, every individual is a divine prism reflecting not only physical traits but soul power as well—that is, not only who we are now but who we can become when we live to our fullest potential. Ultimately, it takes seeing ourselves from the perspective of both the head and the heart to obtain a more expanded and integrated view of ourselves.

When both partners release patterns that impede the full self-expression of their beings, they move beyond mirroring each other's superficial patterns to a shared experience of being, which opens them to a new joy in living. Then they can exude this vital energy while walking the dog, talking to the grocery store clerk, cooking dinner together, listening to music, or traveling. Seen from this vantage point, relationships are opportunities for both self-realization and partnership transformation.

### *Using Shared Expanded Conscious Awareness*

Like the wardrobe in *The Chronicles of Narnia* that transports the children to another world, shared expanded conscious awareness helps soul-hearted partners cocreate a new reality together. In one sense, sharing their intuitions, sensations, and experiences with each other contributes to a broader perspective for both, as if experiencing life through four eyes instead of two. In another sense, using shared expanded conscious awareness is like building a house and standing with your partner on the top floor without the roof yet in place, and seeing the entire expanse from a three-hundred-and-sixty-degree perspective. In contrast, viewing life without such awareness is like being able to see only through the doors and windows, giving a unidimensional perspective.

In soul-hearted partnership, we create an observation deck at the heart level, showing us many more possibilities in each moment than we could otherwise envision. The walls that once obstructed our view dissolve, and we can see life from the perspective of our combined hearts. In her poem "Rain in May", Jane Hirshfield expresses the essence of this broader and more variegated perspective: "To hear as a sand crab hears the waves, loud as a second heart; to see as a green thing sees the sun, with the undividing attention of blind love."[3]

While using expanded conscious awareness as partners, we still remain open to the information spirit gives us to guide our individual choices, such as changing careers, furthering our education, pursuing a creative endeavor, or starting a business that may result in a relocation. In such circumstances, it is important that partners trust each other to act on this guidance with love and consideration for each other and the partnership. In addition, partners need to be flexible in negotiating changes that stretch them spiritually, and thus require support.

The value of partners using shared expanded conscious awareness to align intentions and make discerning choices is illustrated by the following story. I encouraged my clients Margo and Todd to be attuned to each other by opening their hearts, trusting the information they received about themselves and their relationship, and sharing it with each other. While practicing these principles, they were presented with a chance to be sole investors in and executive producers of an independent film project. Despite having little experience in the entertainment industry, they were drawn to the opportunity.

As Margo sat in the business meeting discussing the contract with their new business partners, she experienced tension in her solar plexus and a strong feeling of uneasiness. She had an intuitive sense that the people with whom they were developing the contract were not trustworthy and lacked integrity, and felt that she and Todd should walk away from the project. Afraid of disappointing Todd, however, she let him go ahead and negotiate terms. Within a few months, Margo's intuition was validated when the director of the film breached the contract by making a poor quality film, keeping the video equipment for himself and, without Margo and Todd's permission, copying parts of the film to use in another project.

Although the project didn't become the financial success Margo and Todd had dreamed, it had given them significant information about themselves and their relationship. First, Margo saw that she had to trust herself and share her insights with Todd no matter how afraid she was of disappointing or displeasing him. Todd, on the other hand, realized he needed to trust Margo's intuition as much as his own. Together, they learned to use their shared expanded conscious awareness, which ultimately resulted in Todd's leaving his current management position to become a business consultant and author, and Margo deciding to return to graduate school and follow her dream of becoming a teacher.

Aligning and making discerning choices to support our intentions with a partner leads to endless acts of cocreation. In facing these new possibilities, it is important to be flexible and view mistakes as opportunities for spiritual growth. Maintaining this perspective helps us eliminate polarized patterns of right/wrong, good/bad, and win/lose and allows for spontaneity upon receiving spiritual guidance.

The following story illustrates how we can learn to use our shared expanded conscious awareness to manifest our intentions as individuals or a couple. In planning a recent trip to Istanbul, Turkey, Doug and I had spent hours researching travel sites, blogs, and books on Turkish carpets and how to purchase a quality carpet from a reputable dealer. But what began as a shared intention to enjoy buying a Turkish rug together soon deviated into a determined effort to bring home a museum-quality rug at a rock-bottom price.

Expecting a enjoyable shopping spree, we began our search for carpets the day after we arrived in Istanbul. Escorted to the back showrooms of carpet stores, given Turkish tea, and shown rug after rug, we ended up investing much time and energy in what soon became a frustrating enterprise. Feeling at one location that we were never going to get out the door unless we bought a carpet, we contemplated just picking one to finish the arduous process. Yet that was not what the universe had in store for us.

During our last day in Istanbul, as we were sitting on our rooftop terrace having breakfast, I said to Doug, "Since we've put all this time and energy into finding a carpet, I want to go home with a Turkish carpet one way or another." Doug realized how our intention had shifted from having an enjoyable experience to being obsessed with the outcome and that I had slipped into my past pattern of control, attempting to manifest our intention through sheer force of will. Doug knew that at this point he had to detach himself from my reaction, not take it personally, and just allow the experience to unfold.

Later that morning we passed a government store that sold sub—museum quality Turkish carpets at fixed prices with no haggling. Without hesitation we found a carpet that was acceptable and at a fair price; however, we both knew it wasn't what we really wanted. Realizing that my need for control was driving my behavior, I decided to take a break and walked out of the store. Doug quickly caught up to me, asked me to slow down and breathe, and inquired, "Do you really want to settle for this carpet?" "No," I answered, "but it is the carpet that is available at the right price right now." Then he gently suggested that we return to Kalite, one of the stores we had visited earlier in the week, where we had seen several carpets we liked. Still entrenched in my pattern of control, I felt a need to buy this carpet once and for all and returned to the government store.

As I pondered the item, I heard the voice of spirit whisper, "Kalite," but ignoring it I told the clerk I wanted to buy the carpet.

As they carried it to the counter, I slumped down into a chair, hoping to feel relieved. But instead, I felt more agitated, so I asked Doug if he would handle the transaction. I watched as the store clerk tried to jam the folded carpet into a tiny plastic bag and secure the bag with plastic tape. As the sound of the crackly tape became louder and more irritating, I felt like the magic carpet I had been floating on was being pulled out from under me.

Recognizing these as spiritual cues guiding me to follow my heart, I finally blurted out, "Stop." As I felt more grounded, I was able to ask the clerk, "Where is the certificate of authenticity that accompanies this carpet?" Once I saw that they were unable to produce the certificate of authenticity, I knew I had to be true to myself and not buy something I did not really want.

As Turkish security was called to handle the refund, Doug quietly said he would finish the transaction and that I could wait outside. But I knew I needed to see this embarrassing process through with courage and grace. As they started to unroll the rug and scratch a large, bold X across the VAT tax form, I looked at Doug with gratitude for his earlier attempt to alert me that I wasn't being true to myself. As we stepped outside the store, I thanked him for supporting my choices without blame or judgment. His genuine love had assisted me in seeing that I could let go of the old choice and make a new one.

After he again suggested we return to Kalite, I agreed. When we entered the store, we were clear in our shared intention to enjoy the possibilities presented to us, with the attitude of "let's see what happens." As a result, not only did we enjoy ourselves but we found a carpet we loved and that was within our price range and exhibited the craftsmanship we wanted.

As is exemplified by this story, looking at any experience through shared expanded conscious awareness helps us perceive options we are unable to see alone. Such experiences help us build trust in ourselves, each other, and the relationship. To do this consistently, we must view life from a more spiritual perspective, eliminate the expectation of particular outcomes, and be willing to work together in uncharted territory.

Signs that partners are sharing conscious awareness include, for example, finding themselves speaking at the same time, finishing each other's sentences, having the same feeling or thought simultaneously, or having an intention to do something then discovering their partner has done it for them. Imagine craving oysters and your partner comes home from work with oysters, or thinking about getting the light fixed on the deck, only to find that your partner has already called the electrician. In such situations, your use of expanded conscious awareness already has you and your partner in sync with each other.

To enhance this level of spiritual attunement, it is essential for couples to release negative behavioral patterns since, like steam on a bathroom mirror that keeps us from seeing our true being, they block the partners' creative flow of energy. In addition, breaking old habits can instill within the partners much welcome spontaneity.

Using shared conscious awareness allows partners to clearly communicate, release reactions, and remain responsive to each other. They can then avoid situations that might trigger old patterns or even negative parts of their history together. In this way, they can head off problems that are likely to disrupt the flow of creative energies needed to sustain their soul-hearted partnership.

## Shared Recognition and Release of Patterns

In the mirror of relationships we can often see old patterns surface. As they come into the light of our conscious awareness and we attune to the voice of spirit, we may become aware of valuable opportunities for releasing those that drain energy from our relationships. Our cherished relationships offer even more, for they help us look clearly and deeply at patterns that need to be changed so we can realize our fullest potential.

Cocreators of soul-hearted partnerships especially need to vigilantly take responsibility for recognizing and releasing debilitating patterns. As if old patterns were hats, when they surface partners need to hang them back on the hat rack, supported nonjudgmentally in releasing them so the two can continue maintaining a fulfilling soul-hearted partnership. As Danish philosopher Søren Kierkegaard advises, in his book *Works of Love*, "It is not you who, on the grounds of the weakness of the beloved, are to remove yourself, as it were, from him or make your relationship more distant; on the contrary, the two are to hold together all the more firmly and inwardly in order to remove the weakness."[4]

To support each other in releasing patterns, partners first have to establish enough openness and trust to feel safe revealing these self-destructive behaviors to each other. Second, upon noticing a behavior that signals a partner's old pattern, it is considered the person's responsibility to bring it to their partner's attention and for the partner to welcome the information. In becoming jointly aware of cues that signal the emergence of old patterns, partners are to avoid bickering, defensiveness, or lack of resolution about past issues—an outcome best served when a person's urge to blame, resent, or attack their partner is replaced by courteous words and understanding, letting them know a pattern has surfaced. A truly compassionate partner is one who never stops seeing the beauty of the other's being even when the individual's personality is entrenched in patterns. They feel no need to rescue them or resolve their problems because they see them as strong, capable, and competent in caring for themselves.

Third, partners must be fully present with each other to facilitate recognition and release of all thoughts, feelings, and choices associated with patterns, without guilt or judgment, to clear a path for the evolution of the relationship. Unfortunately, in many relationships people are overwhelmed by cues alerting them to the reemergence of a pattern and frequently react by blaming or attacking the other person rather than recognizing and releasing the pattern. In such situations, failure to release the pattern interrupts the flow of creative energy that feeds the spiritual growth of the couple and ultimately undermines their communication and trust.

Intimate partners are not immune to finding fault with each other rather than working together to recognize and release their patterns. For instance, the pattern of right/wrong, which operates in all human relationships, often comes to light when partners with different driving styles become backseat drivers. In this scenario, the passenger may make what she regards as a neutral comment about her partner's driving, such as "You may want to slow down," which is then taken as criticism. The driver, feeling worthless and coming to his own defense, reacts in an outburst of anger. Instead of realizing a pattern has emerged, the passenger then reacts to the driver's reaction, trying to deflect her own feelings of inadequacy by saying to her partner, "Why are you so defensive?" The driver gets emotional and reacts back, saying, "Why are you so critical?" Such a situation, in which both partners feel criticized and worthless, lacks a constructive resolution.

We often find fault with our partner because it makes us momentarily feel right or in control and distracts us from our own fears and insecurities. In self-righteously judging or attacking our partner, however, we instill an atmosphere of criticism into the partnership. In contrast, we can pause, recognize our pattern or reaction, and refrain from using any defensive or critical words. We can then resume the conversation by listening with an open heart, accepting the other person's experience, and resolving the issue without finding blame.

Recognizing and releasing the need for control can occur when one partner offers to make breakfast, clean the house, or handle finances for the other, who, overriding the impulse to give directions on how to do it their way, graciously accepts and yields to their partner's way. In this instance the focus shifts from judgment to gratitude—extended to the partner both for doing the task and also for helping to recognize and release the pattern of control.

Another example of how partners can work together to recognize and release patterns is the following scenario. Imagine your partner calls you while you are in the middle of completing a household task and asks you to bring a bottle of wine to a cookout you are both attending later that day. You quickly agree but forget to make a note to yourself. Arriving at the party, you remember the bottle of wine and, awash in feelings of inadequacy, you start berating yourself for being forgetful. When your partner asks you for the wine, you react defensively, not wanting to deal with their disappointment. In reaction, your partner self-righteously reminds you that they had to remember everything else and all you had to think about was the wine.

Before the situation escalates further, you can pause, walk away if necessary, and observe the reemergence of old patterns of self-righteousness and avoidance. Then, instead of becoming defensive or waiting to be attacked all over again, forgive yourself for the mistake and immediately acknowledge it to your partner. Your partner, in turn, can refrain from pointing out more instances showing how irresponsible you are, whereupon you can enter into peaceful problem-solving by offering to buy a bottle of wine or drinking the wine that is already at the party. Feeling supported, your partner apologizes, and you hold yourself accountable for your mistake, vowing that next time you will be sure to make a note about any such request.

When both partners respond peacefully by not taking each other's reaction personally, an opportunity arises for spiritual growth. This can occur when, after a confrontation, you ask your partner if they want to clear what transpired—that is, if they would set aside some quiet time during which you could ask permission to speak freely from your heart and offer supportive feedback about what you observed. In the event that you and your partner are open and share responsibility equally, such an exchange would allow you to come together to enhance your spiritual growth.

In preparing for such constructive exchanges, it is essential for both partners to practice asking for permission to speak freely, which alerts one partner that the other wants to be open about a situation without being seen as critical and gives the other partner a chance to prepare to receive supportive feedback. Announcing the open discussion in advance gives each partner time to absorb new information without feeling blamed or judged.

Then, the positive sharing of observations or advice not only initiates the recognition and release of patterns but also provides an opportunity for mutual support. In doing this, you may find that a troublesome pattern resolves on its own, largely because you and your partner, seeing that the destructive pattern has nothing to do with the person's true being takes responsibility for clearing it in order to spiritually progress. Thus clear communication is as essential with yourself as it is with your partner.

Clearing an emotional confrontation in this way helps partners recognize the surfacing of a pattern from the earliest hint of annoyance, which makes it easier to release the behavior and prevent it from triggering another confrontation. The clearing also reorients partners to the present moment so they can respond from their hearts rather than from their past habitual reactions. Then, through open and clear communication, they can keep the flow of positive energy circulating and producing solutions for disagreements, encouraging them to stretch spiritually instead of reinforcing unresolved issues and negative patterns.

Guidelines for recognizing and releasing patterns in a relationship include the following. First, be aware of how you and your partner's verbal and nonverbal language alert you to any negative mindsets, beliefs, and patterns. Phrases such as "You always," "You never," "You make me feel," or "You are like your mother" can undermine an open and honest discussion with each other. It is far more effective to use I-statements, such as "I observed," "I sensed," or "I felt," to alert your partner to a pattern that has surfaced. Using I-statements will help your partner flag patterns in a compassionate way, asking themselves: "Do I make assumptions, presumptions, and generalizations without checking in with my partner?" and "Does my tone of voice or choice of words sound critical, harsh, or self-righteous?" If you feel your partner is using a critical or self-righteous tone or making a mean-spirited comment, call attention to it and ask them to stop immediately, even if your partner does not share your experience.

Second, trust your own experience and share what you are observing or feeling with your partner so that you can immediately clear whatever patterns or grievances have surfaced. When you or your partner sense a change in mood or behavior, pause and check in with each other. Be aware of any couple triggers, verbal or nonverbal, that touch on a sensitive issue, inciting conflict between the two of you—and choose a code word that alerts you to the fact that such a topic has surfaced. Then use this code word to table a discussion or stop an activity until you can be receptive to each other's point of view. Use of the code word can help you avoid repeating previous circular debates and inspire new conversation.

For instance, Susan and Andrea decided on a code word "Katie," that alerted them when an unresolved issue, or couple trigger, emerged that usually caused a circular argument often resulting in anger and disappointment. In past discussions, their couple pattern had been that Andrea made a negative comment or became judgmental of Susan's past relationship with her ex-girlfriend, and in return, Susan reacted defensively by withdrawing or avoiding the topic. Ultimately, they learned that as this issue surfaced, they needed to table the discussion until they could listen to each other's point of view and express their feelings openly without fear of judgment.

Third, use humor as a way of letting your partner know that you have noticed a pattern has surfaced. For example, when I fall into a pattern of self-righteousness, my husband lovingly teases me by imitating the haughty walk I engaged in while trying to flag down a cab in Rome. Recalling this funny moment on a vacation breaks the tension, calls attention to the pattern, and encourages me to take myself less seriously. When you can laugh at your own imperfections, you know you are releasing them, which boosts the flow of positive energy in the relationship.

Finally, realize that when there has been, or you anticipate, a major change, it is likely to cause a pattern to surface—an event for which you can be prepared. For instance, any information signaling that you and your partner are going through a transition or about to realize a dream may trigger a pattern. This is because of the increased vulnerability that is present when we are fulfilling our soul potential. In such situations, acknowledge that you feel a shift and positively channel your energies through your heart to manifest your intention.

Following these guidelines for recognizing and releasing patterns in a soul-hearted partnership increases the opportunities for partners to interact being-to-being in the present rather from a set of behavioral patterns tied to the past. Arresting patterns as partners takes open, clear communication, continuous practice, and loving mutual support. And being willing to constantly peel away the layers of existing patterns will lead to the evolution of a more fulfilling partnership.

**Soul-hearted partnership encourages us to share higher levels of conscious awareness so that we can use our combined energies to make more dis-**

cerning choices. It necessitates being responsible for how we perceive and respond to life's circumstances no matter what is happening. As loving partners, we have to release any negative patterns that inhibit trust or interfere with open and clear communication. Then together we can direct the flow of shared energies toward maintaining a soul-hearted partnership that transcends the bounds of any relationship we have ever imagined.

## PRACTICING THE PRINCIPLES IN CHAPTER SEVEN

1. *Recognize that every relationship you become involved in provides you with valuable information about yourself and your patterns.* Practice using relationships as a mirror for recognizing your negative thoughts, mindsets, and beliefs by asking: "What do my interactions with this person tell me about my own reactivity?" "How do I see myself when I look in the mirror of my relationships?" and "What spiritual information do I glean about myself that I can apply in my life?"

2. *Keep a relationship journal in which you acknowledge the experiences you share with your partner.* Write to each other in this journal, expressing your love and humor. Also jot down experiences to open a dialogue on issues that are hard to discuss in person, or to ask your partner for supportive feedback. When you are both ready, have an openhearted discussion with each other.

3. *Practice using expanded conscious awareness with your partner.* Choose an intention that you wish to cocreate together. Then open your hearts and expand your conscious awareness to view all possibilities. Observe any new information you receive from this broad perspective. Listen to the voice of spirit, and share any information you receive from this dimension as well. Expanding your conscious awareness together reinforces your ability to be open, in sync, and make discerning choices to manifest shared intentions.

4. *Practice recognizing and releasing patterns with your partner.* Be aware of cues, such as bickering and blaming, that indicate a pattern has surfaced. Use a code word or phrase, such as "Stop," "Break," or "Time out," to alert each other to the emergence of a couple trigger that could cause an argument. Set aside time to discuss the issue without interruption, listening fully to each other's point of view.

5. *Solicit assistance from others whose points of view are trustworthy to evaluate your own and your partner's patterns.* Broaden your perspective on sources of your patterns by talking to friends or a therapist.

# Chapter Eight

## Soul-Hearted Partnership As the Shared Expression of Unconditional Love

"Love one another, but make not a bond of love:
let it rather be a moving sea between the shores of your souls."

—KAHLIL GIBRAN

WHEN TWO INDIVIDUALS CONNECT heart to heart and soul to soul, they share a reservoir of energy expressed as unconditional love with each other and experience a transcendent level of relationship. This experience can be compared to the interaction of two professional dancers, alternately leading and supporting the other, each bringing energy and capability so the dance flows gracefully and effortlessly. Living in a soul-hearted partnership means being able to unite the energy of our being with that of a partner to participate in elevated life experiences. When we make a commitment to soul-hearted partnership, we join in a blissful union, in which each partner loves beyond self and the other, experiencing unconditional love of all beings.

### Seeing Soul-Hearted Partnership As a Sacred Covenant

Soul-hearted partnership is more than an agreement to share life together; it is a sacred covenant that partners make with each other to express their fullest selves regardless of their life circumstances. Like surfing, we ride the crest of the waves and allow for bumps and falling off the board at times. But maintaining a seamless energetic flow no matter what life presents, individually or in relationship, is what sustains such a partnership.

Seeing soul-hearted partnership as a sacred covenant that we enter into with ourselves and our chosen partner underscores the depth of love, trust, intimacy, commitment, and mutual respect needed to cocreate and sustain such a relationship. There are no limits to the peace, joy, and well-being that manifests through this kind of relationship. With this beloved partner, we feel emotionally and spiritually strengthened and uplifted beyond our physical limitations.

The sacred covenant of soul-hearted partnership is founded on the following unspoken vows that are exchanged heart to heart: "I am asking you to give up holding back any part of yourself. I am asking you to fully participate in our relationship and in life without reservation, and to be uninhibited. I am asking you for the deepest level of love, trust, and intimacy. I am asking you to be open, present, and aware, without playing roles or games. I want you to see me as the beloved partner you have always wanted and live your life with no excuses and no regrets expressed by 'If only' and 'What if.'"

The following story illustrates how our intention to enter into the sacred covenant of soul-hearted partnership can help deepen love, trust, intimacy, and commitment on all levels. In celebration of our upcoming marriage, Doug and I wanted to enter into a sacred covenant by exchanging vows honoring our partnership. Our shared intention was to create an intimate ceremony in Italy that expressed our loving connection as physical beings, kindred spirits, and soul-hearted mates. Consequently, we opted not to have my two children or our immediate families attend but instead to share our joy with family and friends by having a post-wedding celebration upon returning home from our honeymoon.

Our wedding in Florence, Italy, was the ultimate experience of soul-hearted partnership as a sacred covenant. In keeping with our new beginnings, it took place in a foreign country, in a foreign language, and with foreigners as our witnesses. In an intimate ceremony in a medieval castle, we spoke our spontaneous vows to each other, promising to share the fullest expression of ourselves with one another.

A week later, in Paris, we united spiritually in a playful ceremony that took place on a stone bench in a museum courtyard. With music in the background and children playing, we pledged our connection to each other as kindred spirits and lovingly exchanged the divine energy that flowed through each of our hearts to one heart.

Topping it all off, we joined soulfully in the chapel of Sainte-Chapelle in Paris. Standing in the chapel, with its floor-to-ceiling stained-glass windows illuminated by the sun, we felt like we were in a jewel box that reflected the richness of our partnership. Feeling the vibration of our energies moving through our hearts, we affirmed our soul connection and made a sacred vow to sustain our partnership. Bathed in the kaleidoscopic effect of colors, we transcended our physical relationship and entered into the covenant of soul-hearted partnership.

Subsequently, each year on our wedding anniversary we usually travel to some destination with spiritual connections to enter into a new sacred covenant with each other. This annual celebration provides an opportunity to reflect on the previous year, spiritually connect, and consciously prepare our intentions for the coming year.

For our first anniversary, Doug and I set a shared intention to manifest a Peruvian shamanic ceremony as the backdrop for the exchange of our vows. Once we arrived in Machu Picchu, we worked with the hotel staff to set up a sacred sun ceremony with a native shaman from the village. The evening before our anniversary, however, the shaman canceled. Had we expected the shamanic ceremony to be the only way to celebrate our partnership, we would have been disappointed. But trusting our ability to cocreate, we let go of having this particular ceremony and opened to the possibility of a different event.

At sunrise on our anniversary, we entered Machu Picchu and proceeded to the ancient sundial where we spoke our vows. When we climbed to the top of the ruins where the sundial was located, we noticed an older native Peruvian man taking a collection of items out of a brightly colored pouch and arranging them on the flat surface of the sundial. We suddenly realized that he was a shaman preparing to hold the sacred Inca sun ceremony. We quietly waited, watching the sun's rays pass through the V-shaped gap in the mountain and intersect with the surface of the sundial. Once the shaman looked in the direction of the sun and began chanting, Doug and I faced each other, joined in the ceremony, and dedicated our love and lives to each other.

After the exchange of our vows, the shaman approached us and performed a traditional Inca blessing for our union. He gave each of us tobacco leaves over which to declare an intention before throwing them to the wind. Later, we discovered that this native man was a prominent shaman in Peru, professor at a prestigious university, and an expert in performing the Inca sacred sun ceremony. By releasing all expectations and trusting the flow of our energies even when it seemed like things weren't going our way, we manifested our intention better than we had even dreamed. This experience affirmed for us that seeing soul-hearted partnership as a sacred covenant can help reinforce trust, love, and commitment as a foundation for cocreation.

## The Mutual Exchange of Unconditional Love

The mutual exchange of unconditional love propels the shared experience of soul-hearted partnership forward. Its energy radiates through us when we open our hearts to ourselves, another person, and life itself. The partners are not dependent on each other for love, but together they can intensify love and light energy in the universe. In *Letters to a Young Poet*, Rainer Maria Rilke comments on how such love compels us to become more compassionate human beings: "Love is a high inducement for individuals to ripen, to strive to mature in the inner self, to become world, to manifest maturity in the outer world, to become that manifestation for the sake of another." [1]

This environment of unconditional love creates a safe haven in which the partners can freely express themselves, both individually and as a couple, knowing that their weaknesses and imperfections will not be judged or criticized but mutually transformed. Such a nurturing environment supports a mutual state of openheartedness in which we can expose to our partner our patterns and vulnerabilities, as well as the essence of our true being. When we genuinely love another person, we see our light reflected in their face.

The exchange of unconditional love is also described as an experience in which everything takes on an iridescent glow or as a feeling of life as enhanced. For example, we see such reciprocal energy when a baby lights up as her parent enters the room. Similarly, when we see our light reflected in the face of a beloved partner, we naturally draw the light consciously to us.

Many of us find giving and receiving unconditional love difficult, especially when we let the irritations of daily life—such as the hair left in the shower drain, or the overdraft in the checking account—block the flow of this energy. It is not easy to sustain unconditional love for a partner when an individual lets the details of life get in the way and ceases to focus on the more fluid perspective of life as a series of changes leading to growth. This challenge is described by Anne Morrow Lindbergh in her book *Gift from the Sea*: "When you love someone, you do not love them all the time, in exactly the same way, from moment to moment. It is an impossibility. It is even a lie to pretend to. And yet, this is exactly what most of us demand. We have so little faith in the ebb and flow of life, of love, of relationships. We leap at the flow of the tide and resist in terror its ebb. We are afraid it will never return. We insist on permanency, on duration, on continuity; when the only continuity possible, in life as in love, is in growth, in fluidity—in freedom, in the sense that the dancers are free, barely touching as they pass, but partners in the same [soul space]." [2]

The mutual exchange of unconditional love in soul-hearted partnership motivates both partners to interact without expectations or any sense of obligation that might inhibit freedom of self-expression. For instance, you observe that your partner could use a break from getting up early in the morning with the new puppy. Although you both had agreed it would be your partner's responsibility to take care of the puppy, you rise early every now and then to give your partner that much-needed respite. Or your partner, suspecting you have had a stressful day at work, has prepared dinner and a bath to welcome you home. A few hours before serving dinner, your partner finds out that your son is coming over and bringing his girlfriend; instead of getting upset about the last-minute notice, your partner remains flexible, knowing that seeing your son is important to you. Or realizing your desire to spend more time with your teenage daughter, your partner surprises you by arranging a weekend trip with her to New York City. Such random acts of kindness are performed free of obligation, with the understanding that the positive energy they generate comes back to you, your partner, and the relationship a thousandfold.

The story of my clients Ben and Julia provides an example of how unconditional love can be expressed through random acts of kindness that nurture both partners' freedom of self-expression. Ben gifted Julia with enrollment in a cooking class taught by one of her favorite local chefs because he knew that it was among her most enjoyable creative outlets. One evening after the class she arrived home beaming with exuberance—an enthusiasm that inspired Ben, ignited an arousing conversation, and led to passionate lovemaking.

Stimulated by the passionate exchange of their energies, Ben revealed to Julia his dream of filmmaking. This gave her the idea to gift him with a computer class so he could follow his passion. After a series of classes, he excitedly compiled a video photo album of their travel adventures. Their loving exchange supported their individual and shared intentions as well as their soul-hearted partnership.

As illustrated by Ben's and Julia's actions, by honoring and accepting our partner's experience in any given moment, we acknowledge their trust in their own true being. And although we can never have our partner's experience, we can share it with them. We can also support our partner's ability to make choices without interference. In doing so, and not taking our partner's choices personally, we afford our partner the freedom to make choices without obligation. For example, suppose your partner has been in an unhealthy relationship with work, and although you may feel that a career change would be best, instead you listen, offer your point of view if asked, and rather than reacting, actively reinforce your partner's ability to resolve the situation, without judgment or attachment to any outcome. In such situations, we support our partner through holding the space of unconditional love while at the same time giving them the freedom to absorb the information being presented to them and to make their own choices. Later in *Letters to a Young Poet*, Rainer Maria Rilke illuminates the challenge of holding the space of unconditional love: "For one human being to love another is perhaps the most difficult task of all, the epitome, the ultimate test. It is that striving for which all other striving is merely preparation."[3]

Holding the space of unconditional love requires that we remain fully present, keep our hearts open, and accept our partner and their experiences. In this way, we demonstrate no investment in a particular outcome, permitting our partner to let down their guard, open their heart, and allow their patterns to surface and be resolved. In return, we receive from our partner the gratitude that comes when resistance is eliminated and unconditional love prevails.

When we release resistance, struggle ceases and we keep the shared positive flow of energy from being blocked so it continues to support the fullest expression of our individual beings and the relationship. As a result, the integrity of the relationship is maintained, the energy that sustains it expands, and a mutual exchange of unconditional love occurs. In releasing resistance to our partner's preferences, we are also more likely to genuinely accept their experiences without fear or upset. Using expanded conscious awareness, we can quickly move beyond any patterns and become receptive to their choices without blame, judgment, or resentment.

The following example illustrates how holding the space of unconditional love fosters open and clear communication and generates a win-win-win situation for both partners individually and their relationship. Peter sensed a decrease of physical intimacy in his relationship with Jennifer, as she increased the amount of time and energy she spent focused on creative writing. Choosing to be a supportive and loving partner, he temporarily took on the majority of household and parenting duties. He made this choice freely, feeling no obligation or expectations of Jennifer and no loss of self but only the desire to support her new passion. He was thus able to honor Jennifer's relationship with herself, as well as maintain the flow of energy in their partnership. But after a while Peter realized that their energies were moving out of alignment. He knew he needed to share his observation honestly with Jennifer so they could bring their partnership back into balance.

During a calm and intimate moment, Peter asked Jennifer for permission to speak freely to her. Because he had opened a dialogue with her in a loving way, free of blame, she was able to listen to his point of view without resistance or defensiveness. His supportive feedback gave her the impetus to look at the possibility that she had been directing most of her energy into fulfilling her own needs, which was throwing their partnership off balance. While still maintaining her full self-expression, she became receptive to adjusting her priorities and sharing more of her time and energy with Peter. Letting go of expectations that their physical intimacy needed to be sexual, they also explored more innovative ways of sustaining emotional intimacy. Consequently, Jennifer received more physical and emotional care from Peter and gave him more attention and nurturing. Making these adjustments supported the continued flow of their combined energies through their partnership.

After a long summer break, Jennifer had the chance to further support Peter in some challenging months as a teacher, by taking care of the household and parenting responsibilities while he focused more of his energies on his job priorities. Maintaining the harmonious flow of their energies depended not on some credit and debit spreadsheet but rather on supporting each other's individual intentions as well as the shared intention of their partnership.

In other words, just because we have given our partner a massage doesn't mean we have to wait until they give us one before we give them another. The important aspect of exchange is the flow of energy, not the form it takes. There is no need to keep track of who did what as we make conscious choices to gift each other.

Since even in a soul-hearted partnership it is challenging to love ourselves or our partner unconditionally for a prolonged period of time, patterns of insecurity can surface unexpectedly when it seems like our partner has hurt or disappointed us. Initially, we may react by withdrawing and becoming defensive. At this point, affirmation of our partner's love for us will allow us to arrest our pattern of insecurity and work through it without feeling judged. Then, given time and space to process our emotional reaction, we will often be able to identify the source of our insecurity, which may be fear of losing our partner's love. In hindsight, we can see that there was no evidence to validate this fear, and in fact our oversensitivity to the situation may indicate that we are harboring resentment or nursing a grievance about someone or something else.

Anytime an issue incites a reaction, we need to give ourselves permission to pause, stop replaying past files, and shift from being reactive to being responsive. Such a purposeful break can keep us from taking our partner's venting or other disappointing behavior personally. It also helps to remember to accept responsibility for ourselves and let our partner deal with their own reactions. In maintaining this sort of healthy detachment, infused with unconditional love, we can even become a valuable sounding board for our partner. Operating in this way makes us feel more centered and our partner feel more secure in articulating their concerns. When both partners are fully present, they are free to consider new information that can facilitate open discussion, the release of emotional reactivity, and the birth of an inspired experience.

Expressing unconditional love is especially important when partners are apart or engaging in separate activities. When apart, it is necessary for partners to sustain complete trust in and love of each other beyond doubt and fear. One way to do this is by trusting that we are in constant energetic communication with our partner as we think of them throughout the day. Moreover, we have to trust that our relationship is secure. For instance, while traveling separately we can demonstrate unconditional love by appreciating but not needing or expecting periodic phone calls or contact from our partner. It is important to acknowledge our need to feel loved and supported by our partner, without placing demands or blame.

An environment of unconditional love will facilitate the release of any pattern that can undermine a soul-hearted partnership because, by contrast, it makes partners acutely aware of times when their patterns of neediness, insecurity, and abandonment arise. For example, while on a business trip your partner calls to talk and catches you distracted, unable to relate to them, seemingly distant or uninterested. Taking your aloofness personally, your partner feels hurt and disappointed. From your perspective, you are distracted because you are taking care of a child at that moment, and you become annoyed with your partner's pattern of insecurity and need for reassurance. In this case, it is important for you to clearly communicate to your partner that you love them and it's not a good time for chitchat. On the other hand, it is just as critical for your partner to flag their pattern of insecurity and refrain from projecting such negative energy in the future. Together you can acknowledge that insecurity does not support the growth of your partnership, but building trust does. To build trust, you can practice calling each other without any agenda other than to express love. Also, you can agree that if one of you is unavailable when the other partner calls, the caller will not take it personally or jump to any conclusions.

Trusting that a relationship is secure does not, however, mean taking each other or the relationship for granted. Unfortunately, when we are in a relationship that is safe we often feel free to do things that may hurt or demean our partner, such as venting or making mean-spirited, sarcastic comments. The old adage "Familiarity breeds contempt" is too often true in relationships. Complacency is a lethal pattern that will drain any relationship of the energy to spiritually progress. Even in relationships built on a foundation of absolute trust and unconditional love, partners must maintain respect for each other regardless of the circumstances.

In a world where most people's experience of love is conditional, it is vital that partners express unconditional love no matter how challenging the times may be. In a soul-hearted partnership, every discussion should begin with an acknowledgment of the other person, such as "I love you" or "I'm here for you." This flow of energetic support is demonstrated by constant consideration. As partners, you complement each other, embodying a powerful energetic support team.

## Forgiveness As an Act of Unconditional Love

Forgiveness is an act of unconditional love in which an individual focuses their energy through their heart center then blesses and releases anything that does not align with their true being. Forgiveness as a spiritual practice transforms patterns of judgment and criticism into compassion and acceptance. Harboring grievances or resentments against a partner fosters negativity and binds the relationship in patterns, so we have to be willing to forgive our partner and the past. Forgiveness only occurs if we truly let go and choose to make the past, with its disappointments, powerless over our lives. Using the mantra "Bless and release" serves the purpose well.

In the safe environment of soul-hearted partnership, partners can help each other heal and grow spiritually through mutual forgiveness. The relationship is further transformed when they forgive the past on a continuing basis by expressing unconditional love. Like a phoenix rising out of the ashes, they can create a new form of a relationship each time they relinquish an old template.

To begin such a new relationship experience, we have to periodically look upon our partner as if for the first time. Most people say hello and good-bye in their relationships, but by continuously transforming themselves and the relationship, soul-hearted partners intermittently say hello, good-bye, and hello again. Seeing the relationship as a series of beginnings and endings, they perpetually create a new relationship from the old one.

The following story illustrates how forgiveness as an act of unconditional love can catalyze the creation of a new relationship from an old one. Chris and Joseph had been married for over seven years, primarily functioning according to prescribed roles and routines, when Chris's father suddenly died. Not having resolved her estrangement from her father before his death sent Chris into a depression.

One night Chris lay alone sprawled on the cold tile of their bathroom floor, feeling like she would never stop crying. While praying to God for help, she gained the insight that it was time to change her life. Chris's prayer was answered when the next day a friend gave her my card and she made an appointment. Through our therapeutic work together, she began grieving her losses, forgiving her past, and engaging in a partnership with herself and her energetic support team. As a result, the patterns in her relationship with her husband became more apparent to her, prompting within her the desire for a more spiritually aware and loving partnership with him.

Initially, Joseph felt paralyzed witnessing Chris's grieving process and depression. His feelings of inadequacy about his ability to support her caused his old pattern of avoidance to surface. Consequently, he distracted himself with video games, Internet surfing, and television, keeping his distance as he always did in situations that made him emotionally uncomfortable. As a result, Chris felt betrayed by the one person who professed to love her and whose support she desperately needed. She believed that if Joseph really loved her he would pay closer attention to her feelings of loss and depression. Instead, Joseph ran from any opportunity for emotional and spiritual intimacy, reinforcing her feelings of insecurity and abandonment.

At a crossroads from which she knew there was no turning back, Chris realized she had to be proactive in healing herself and helping to create a new relationship from their old one. Her wholehearted commitment to developing a fully realized relationship with herself put positive pressure on Joseph to spiritually grow as well. She knew if he didn't open his heart, be vulnerable, and begin to do the spiritual work necessary to change his life, their relationship would not survive.

Terrified yet knowing that his relationship with himself and Chris depended on it, Joseph began working with me to release his patterns of avoidance and seeking approval and to learn how he could encourage Chris's transformation as well as his own. First, he had to let go of his belief that Chris would never be satisfied with him. Additionally, he needed to forgive Chris's tendency to find fault with him, feel confident in bringing the pattern to her attention, and not take her disapproval personally. He also had to become more focused on the present and confront his fears and insecurities when they surfaced.

Chris, on the other hand, had to forgive Joseph for having been physically, emotionally, and spiritually unavailable to her in the past and to see him in a new light as he developed a fuller relationship with himself and became a more responsive, communicative, and loving partner. It was also important that she give him the space he needed to change without being intrusive or demanding. In this way, she could create a safe harbor where he could feel vulnerable and discover his true self.

As Chris and Joseph practiced forgiving their past, they realized it would take consistent effort and energy to build a new relationship. For one thing, both of them would have to be dedicated to personal transformation, which would support them to grow individually and as a couple. For another, they had to consistently recognize when they were rehashing the past and continuously forgive former grievances without judgment or blaming. In this way, forgiveness would become an act of unconditional love in their relationship and a catalyst for freedom and openness.

When forgiveness becomes an act of unconditional love in a relationship, the partners experience a greater sense of freedom to communicate and express themselves fully. Ultimately they feel a compelling desire to forge a new relationship offering fresh possibilities for future fulfillment.


*Practicing Continuous Courtship through Spontaneity, Humor, and Play*
Practicing continuous courtship through spontaneity, humor, and play—all launchpads to creativity and spiritual growth—is the key to keeping positive energy flowing in a soul-hearted partnership. Because society generally frowns upon adults being spontaneous and playful, we can sometimes feel inhibited about expressing ourselves freely. And yet, in following the advice to take life more seriously, grow up, and act like adults, we often lose our sense of life as a passionate adventure to be shared with our partner.

When it comes to being spontaneous, playful, and maintaining a sense of humor in daily life, children are our best teachers, because they endlessly infuse light energy into their encounters. It is important for loving partners to court each other in this childlike spirit every day by doing little things to keep wonder alive, which sustains their soul connection.

Practicing continuous courtship involves doing special things together that support the relationship on all levels—physically, emotionally, and spiritually. Physically, you and your partner could pursue continuous courtship by washing the cars, doing the laundry, gardening, or cooking together playfully instead of individually tackling these household tasks with great earnestness. To nurture your courtship emotionally, strive to be best friends, play together, enjoy each other's company, and take pleasure in such shared experiences as listening to music, having intimate conversations, or watching a sunset. Practicing continuous courtship spiritually means fostering the type of experience Rumi describes in *In the Arc of Your Mallet*: "The way the night knows itself with the moon, be that with me. Be the rose nearest to the thorn that I am. I want to feel myself in you when you taste food, in the arc of your mallet when you work . . ."[4]

Spontaneity, humor, and play naturally open the heart, lift the spirit, and direct our energies to cocreate beyond any limitation, enhancing flexibility, the dissolution of patterns, the elimination of obstacles to full self-expression, and celebration of soulful living. In the state of continuous courtship fed by these elements, we have the sense of riding the crest of a wave, dancing in the light, and being in touch with the oneness of all creation. Flexibility is enhanced because between partners there is no ego, self-consciousness, or reservation but instead naturalness, lightheartedness, and the sense that nothing is more important than the present moment. Laughter comes easily, as does an instantaneous recognition of the absurdity of many situations. For example, you can giggle when you become drenched in an unexpected rain shower while walking the dog, make light of a wrong turn that takes you out of your way, viewing it as a new adventure, and be silly when you arrive late to your destination and have to carry your luggage a mile over cobblestone streets to get to your hotel because you were left at the dock by a water taxi. When such experiences are shared, each partner comes to appreciate the fact that they could not have created them alone but only in concert with a soul-hearted partner as witness.

Spontaneity, humor, and play help dissolve patterns because they encourage us to play along with possibilities. For example, if your partner is excited about the possibility of changing residences or moving to a new state, instead of digging in your heels, dismissing your partner's ideas, and resisting change, you can develop an attitude of "What might that look like?" or "Let's explore the possibility." In the process, you will be supporting what your partner is cocreating and what is opening for you in your relationship together.

In addition, these childlike qualities banish obstacles to self-expression by diffusing feelings of self-consciousness and obligation. As such, we are able to support our partner's silliness and dancing in the dairy aisle of the grocery store even when we wouldn't think of doing it ourselves. In turn, when we sing our favorite song off key while walking in the park with our MP3 player, our partner can humor us or join in. In such moments of full self-expression, there is no room for self-consciousness or obligation—only more spontaneity, humor, and play.

Finally, spontaneity, humor, and play invariably ignite a desire to create celebrations as a means of practicing continuous courtship. We may invent new ways to celebrate our partner and our relationship that are not only fun but also an expression of shared creativity. For example, we might celebrate "birthday seasons" during which we do little things for each other for a week or even a month before or after our actual birthdays. Small gifts that reflect our partner's preferences can be presented to celebrate their true self, such as a sensual massage, a favorite meal, an exquisite wine, flowers, or a promise to take care of all the household chores for the day.

Another way to practice continuous courtship is by sharing creative activities together, such as dance lessons. British journalist Holbrook Jackson suggests: "One should dance because the soul dances."[5] When we dance, we focus on each other so intently that worries and stress disappear and we can let go at the soul level. Similarly, the Romantic poet Lord Byron says: "On with the dance! Let joy be unconfined;/No sleep till morn, when Youth and Pleasure meet/to chase the glowing hours with flying feet."[6] The joy experienced in dancing then spills over into other aspects of our lives. We might dance while making dinner, working in the yard, or walking the dog. As individuals and as a couple, we are designed to be creative, and dance is an engaging means for channeling these energies.

An additional way to practice continuous courtship is by sharing travel experiences. Travel takes us outside of our daily routine, inspiring new avenues of soul-hearted connection. While traveling together, you and your partner could send postcards to each other, write about your shared experiences in a journal, or make a scrapbook about the places you have visited, thereby deepening your relationship. While traveling separately, you can pursue continuous courtship by writing love notes about your partner and tucking them into their purse or suitcase, or by having their favorite wine or food waiting for them when they arrive at their hotel.

When Doug and I travel, we play with unbridled passion. One of our favorite experiences occurred in Paris when we danced under the stars and sang silly songs in the courtyard of the Louvre and then out on the streets. Our state of playfulness, in which we were unconcerned with what others thought or said, led to spontaneous lovemaking. Incidents like this that lighten the heart bring partners closer together.

As we infuse our lives with spontaneity, humor, and play, we experience life from a new perspective, a shared synergy that liberates the body, lightens the heart, and lifts the spirit. Life evolves miraculously when we embrace the philosophy of "Let's see what happens." Making love experientially in everything we do is the ultimate way to practice continuous courtship.


### Sustaining a Heart and Soul Connection

A heart and soul connection nurtures soul-hearted partnership while simultaneously extending the shared expression of unconditional love into the world. Such a connection is fostered through deep physical, emotional, and spiritual intimacy and involves a heightened awareness of a divine union between partners. When we touch each other's heart and soul, we experience reverence, adoration, and deep intimacy. This experience of soul-hearted connection is illuminated by poet e.e. cummings when he says: "here is the deepest secret nobody knows/(here is the root of the root and the bud of the bud/and the sky of the sky of a tree called life;/which grows higher than soul can hope or mind can hide)/ and this is the wonder that's keeping the stars apart/i carry your heart (i carry it in my heart)."[7]

Partners nourish a heart and soul connection by opening their hearts and acknowledging each other on a daily basis, thereby tapping the reservoir of unconditional love and channeling this energy between themselves and out into the world. To cultivate the channeling of light energy back and forth, you could begin each morning by lying in each other's arms, affirming your bond, acknowledging gratitude for your blessings, and sharing your intentions for the day ahead. Then, as the day unfolds you might initiate any conversation with your partner by affirming your heartfelt connection to them or spontaneously call, e-mail, or text message them during the day to say, "I love you" or "I am thinking of you." Sometimes it takes only a heart-felt glance or a twinkle of the eye to acknowledge a heart and soul connection with a partner. The following verse from a poem by Thomas Moore expresses this eloquently: "Love hath a language of his own—A voice, that goes/From heart to heart—whose mystic tone/Love only knows."[8] Pausing to nurture our heart and soul connection at various times during the day allows us to continue perfecting our soul-hearted partnership over time.

To reinforce a heart and soul connection, we must become aware of the behaviors and situations that disrupt this intimate state, such as deceit, mind games, or individuals who are judgmental. Then we can strive to avoid such encounters.

An effective way to reinforce a heart and soul connection is through an exercise I call "soul gazing." To practice this exercise, sit or stand facing your partner and take a few deep breaths together. While inhaling and exhaling, gently cradle your partner's hands and lovingly gaze into their eyes. As you sustain eye contact, open your heart and feel yourself transcending physical form. Now focus this energy heart to heart and release any thoughts that are interrupting this intimate exchange of energy. Experience the circulation of loving energy as it flows from your heart center to your partner's heart center.

Because of the intensity of this circulating energy, it naturally continues outward into the world. Thus in the exquisite space of heart and soul connection, we give and receive unconditional love, both as individuals in a soul-hearted partnership and as humans projecting it out into the world.

**By maintaining a heart and soul connection, combining powerful energies, and expressing unconditional love, we can bring about peace, harmony, and inspiration for ourselves and everyone around us, magnifying the beauty in the world.**

## Practicing the Principles in Chapter Eight

1. *Enter into a sacred covenant of soul-hearted partnership.* Compose partnership vows that can be renewed annually in a special ceremony, using words and phrases that are meaningful to your relationship. Also use these special expressions daily or periodically as reminders of your commitment to each other.

2. *Practice giving and receiving unconditional love.* Nurture unconditional love for your partner by daily or periodically touching your heart center and affirming the unconditional love emanating from you. Give and receive unconditional love without producing mental credit and debit columns. When you give and receive unconditional love continuously without worrying about who gives more, the balance of giving and receiving is naturally resolved over time, and you abide in an openhearted state with each other.

3. *Practice forgiveness as an act of unconditional love.* Consider a hurtful act your partner has committed or attitude your partner has assumed. How do you feel when you think of this situation—anxious, hurt, or perhaps heavy-hearted? If so, acknowledge the grievance without judgment and examine how it intrudes on your interactions with your partner. Use the mantra "Bless and release" to let go of any grievance.

4. *Court your partner daily by engaging in random acts of kindness toward them.* Such acts could include making a special meal with your partner in mind, leaving Post-it love notes that invite your partner to play, giving your partner a massage, preparing a special bath, or unexpectedly arranging for an amazing adventure. Expand on this repertoire periodically to keep magic alive in your relationship.

5. *Use spontaneity, humor, and play to continuously court your partner and dissipate inhibition.* Invent celebratory activities that make you laugh, let go, and play with joyful abandon, such as taking dance lessons, snorkeling, riding bicycles, or traveling.

6. *Nurture your heart and soul connection with your partner through daily rituals of bonding.* Before getting out of bed in the morning, take time to affirm your connection by spending at least a few minutes in each other's arms. Throughout the day, energetically send love to your beloved, using a voice or text message, a written note, or a loving gaze just to say, "I love you and I am thinking of you." Periodically gift yourselves with uninterrupted time together to listen to each other's dreams and aspirations.

7. *Practice sustaining a heart and soul connection with your partner through soul gazing.* Sit or stand facing your partner. Pause and take a few deep breaths together. While inhaling and exhaling, gently cradle your partner's hands and lovingly gaze into their eyes, releasing any thoughts that inhibit the exchange of energy heart to heart. Relax deeply and welcome the presence of unconditional love. Allow the boundaries of your bodies to soften, and melt into each other.

# Chapter Nine

## SOUL-HEARTED PARTNERSHIP AS THE
## SHARED EXPRESSION OF TRUST AND INTIMACY

*"The only real security is not in owning or possessing,*
*not in demanding or expecting, not in hoping, even.*
*Security in a relationship lies neither in looking back to what it was,*
*nor forward to what it might be, but living in the present*
*and accepting it as it is now."*

—ANNE MORROW LINDBERGH

STABLISHING ABSOLUTE TRUST with a partner opens a person to experiencing much deeper levels of intimacy because they then feel safe enough to freely share their fears and insecurities, all the while revealing the core of their being beyond any negative patterns. When absolute trust is an essential element in our partnership, we can more easily let go of everything that impedes the flow of our shared energies. Even when the slightest irritation or conflict occurs, we are not afraid to be vulnerable and to fully express ourselves, listen to our partner's experience, and give supportive feedback. Trusting our conscious awareness, we consistently recognize and release patterns so that we can be receptive to and choose from infinite possibilities in cocreating our life together.

## Reciprocal Absolute Trust

Reciprocal absolute trust solidifies the foundation for soul-hearted partnership because it promotes free expression uninhibited by insecurity and guardedness, and thus open and clear communication. Creating an environment of reciprocal absolute trust with a partner necessitates accepting the relationship for what it is in the present, affirming its spiritual purpose, and avoiding being possessive or fearful of abandonment, so it can evolve. Possessiveness is common among people who suffer insecurity; when their pattern of insecurity is triggered, they tend to judge their partner or become emotionally detached for fear of being hurt or rejected. Both behaviors interrupt the exchange of positive energy and foster an atmosphere of fear and doubt, ultimately causing partners to feel as if they are walking on eggshells.

A partner, especially one fearful of abandonment, may react to this emotional detachment by closing off the flow of energy through their own heart rather than risk rejection. When this happens, the couple begins to relate to each other more from their insecurities than from their true beings, which undermines the integrity of their relationship.

Establishing reciprocal absolute trust requires the ability to consistently recognize and move beyond self-destructive patterns to sustain a steady flow of energy in the relationship. In turn, this flow of energy, one of the greatest gifts of soul-hearted partnership, assures us that our partner's love and nurturing will not disappear, even as the relationship ebbs and flows in keeping with life cycles. Reciprocal absolute trust in soul-hearted partnerships can be likened to a new diver's complete trust in an instructor while learning to scuba dive. The new diver will go to depths of up to sixty feet with their instructor, relying on this person for air and to safely bring them back to the surface. This kind of trust is one we rarely experience in everyday life but desire to have with a partner.

The following story illustrates the evolution of a relationship initially rooted in a lack of reciprocal absolute trust due to patterns of fear and insecurity. Cindy's fear of abandonment began at age ten when her parents divorced and her mother moved away. Later, Cindy's pattern of fear of abandonment affected all her relationships, causing her to either keep people at arm's length or to hold on to them too tightly.

After their first year of marriage, Cindy and Ted had difficulty establishing trust and a deep level of intimacy because they were afraid to be open and honest with each other. While working with them, I observed that Cindy's fear of abandonment caused her to withhold her deepest feelings from Ted. She also felt increasingly more inhibited about revealing her imperfections, afraid that he would discover her faults and leave her, so she shared with him only her superficial thoughts and feelings. She hesitated to "rock the boat" even when it meant taking all the blame for unresolved issues and compromising her own true being, but she did not think twice about attempting to control his every move.

Ted felt smothered by Cindy's fear-based patterns and often overreacted by taking her behavior personally, getting upset, and becoming emotionally detached when she did share her feelings. His own fear of being vulnerable exacerbated his emotional withdrawal, convincing him that he could not receive the love he wanted in the relationship. Having grown up with a father who was never there for him and a mother who was mentally ill, he had learned early on to close off his heart to avoid disappointment and despair. Later, his growing sense of insecurity caused him to withdraw from people and situations before he could be denied love. Eventually, as Ted became better able to enter into intimate conversations without pulling away from Cindy, he learned to face the source of his insecurity and to trust her. At about the same time, Cindy began to realize that when Ted stepped back to explore his feelings and gain clarity, he was not necessarily detaching from her. She then practiced staying more present with him and revealing her deeper feelings when she felt like avoiding them. Consequently, she began to feel secure enough to express her true being without worrying about losing Ted and thus being overly possessive of him.

As illustrated by Cindy and Ted, when both partners have fear-based patterns one partner's pattern can trigger that of the other, resulting in both partners guarding the entrance to their hearts and holding back important information about their true being, inhibiting emotional intimacy. To develop more intimacy, both partners need to build reciprocal absolute trust, release their vice grip on the relationship, and surrender their hearts, thereby opening the flow of loving energy between them. Author Kaleel Jamison eloquently acknowledges the importance of building trust and relinquishing patterns of possessiveness: "Relationships—of all kinds—are like sand held in your hand. Held loosely, with an open hand, the sand remains where it is. The minute you close your hand and squeeze tightly to hold on, the sand trickles through your fingers. You may hold on to some of it, but most will be spilled. A relationship is like that. Held loosely, with respect and freedom for the other person, it is likely to remain intact. But hold too tightly or possessively, and the relationship slips away and is lost."[1]

Upon establishing reciprocal absolute trust in a relationship, we can stop constantly seeking reassurance, which drains it of the creative energy that could be more fruitfully directed. No longer do we have to be always looking over our shoulder, wondering whether any anger, irritability, or expression of displeasure is about the relationship itself. Yet even when we feel secure in such a relationship, we still need to evaluate any information we receive to be sure nothing will erode our hard-won trust.

Some of the most destructive patterns that erode trust in relationship are comparison and jealousy. Patterns of comparison and jealousy usually indicate a lack of self-love and a sense of worthlessness. When we compare ourselves to an external standard or expectation, it is difficult to be ourselves without worrying about whether we appear sufficiently smart, beautiful, or competent. Comparisons to others can incite jealousy, which is among the deadliest patterns that undermine trust in a relationship.

The following story illustrates how one couple recognized a pattern of jealousy that had undermined trust in their relationship. Dawn noticed over the period of several weeks that her husband, Troy, had been making sexual innuendoes and mean-spirited remarks in regard to her relationships with other men, such as friends, doctors, and mentors. He felt insecure because they weren't having sex as often as in the past, and he assumed she must not be physically interested in him anymore or was having an affair. Initially, Dawn felt hurt by Troy's overreaction to their decreased sexual activity because she didn't understand his feelings of insecurity or share this experience. After gaining a broader perspective by using her conscious awareness, however, she was able to acknowledge his insecure feelings, while also recognizing his pattern of jealousy.

Asking for permission to speak freely, Dawn brought the inappropriate comments to Troy's attention. At first, he defensively laughed them off, claiming he had only been joking. Yet as he listened to her supportive feedback he saw that his pattern of jealousy signified a lack of trust in Dawn's love for him.

At the same time, Dawn realized that her recent launching of a new career had channeled most of her energy away from her relationship with her husband. Consequently, she affirmed her love for him and vowed to set aside more time for their relationship. In response, Troy apologized, agreed to express his feelings in a healthy way, and promised to work on releasing his patterns of jealousy and insecurity.

In general, focusing on expectations of having sex in a relationship can indicate a lack of trust. Jumping to the conclusion that not having sex at least twice a week means our partner is not physically attracted to us or is having an affair can put undue pressure on both partners to initiate sex out of obligation. Any time lovemaking becomes routine it drains the creative energies needed to kindle the passion in a relationship. In contrast, having reciprocal absolute trust permits partners to use spontaneity, play, and humor to sustain a continuous courtship.

## Developing Physical, Emotional, and Spiritual Intimacy

Reciprocal absolute trust is the cornerstone for developing intimacy on all levels—physical, emotional, and spiritual. This does not mean both partners must be equally developed on all levels, only that they are open and present on all levels so they will be supported in living in a vulnerable and uninhibited manner. If you feel uncomfortable telling your partner your fears, concerns, or desires, be sure to assess your level of trust in yourself and in the relationship. To attain emotional and spiritual intimacy, we need to be able to freely express ourselves without censorship and listen to our partner without judgment. As Emerson movingly suggests, "Let them be lovers; let them behold truth; and their eyes are uplifted; their wrinkles smoothed, they are perfumed again with hope and power."[2]

Achieving a deeper intimacy on all levels requires taking off our ego-induced armor, surrendering our identity structure, and allowing ourselves to experience unguarded forms of communicating being to being. This can be difficult for many people, however, especially those who perceive themselves as isolated beings, and everyone and everything they encounter as a potential threat that needs to be controlled to ensure their survival. Because of the defense mechanisms created by their ego, such as entitlement and expectations, they are also David with a slingshot ready to slay Goliath whenever or wherever he may appear. Indeed, many of us have learned to act this way habitually, exploding when angry and covering up our wounds through avoidance and denial. Incidents of rage are increasing dramatically on the road, in the workplace, and in homes among otherwise composed individuals. While historically such defensiveness may have aided survival, it is self-destructive and inhibits our ability to develop emotional intimacy.

Barriers to emotional intimacy are often constructed of personal fears. An individual afraid of exposing his vulnerabilities will hide behind his identity structure and shut down his heart. His barriers to intimacy may be further reinforced by difficulties in clear, truthful communication during encounters with people, even his partner, making him feel misunderstood or alienated. For instance, you may be speaking with your partner, feeling the excitement of a stimulating conversation, then without warning your partner, who has had a stressful day and would rather be alone, abruptly reacts with a mean-spirited comment that feels like an arrow piercing your heart. Unprepared for such a reaction, you feel betrayed and realize that you and your partner have been interacting on completely different levels of intimacy, with no true communication going on between you.

Sadly, many partners withdraw from each other at this point with promises to talk later, but one partner may feel too alienated to share deeply with the other. Superficial experiences that ensue may only reinforce this sense of isolation and need to be on guard so as not to suffer further disappointment or hurt. Such conditioning then makes it increasingly difficult for both partners to let down their defenses, so to deepen their intimacy they must learn to overcome this type of conditioning.

Learning how to develop deeper levels of intimacy often necessitates eliminating "emotional baggage" brought to a relationship from past experiences. Most people enter into a relationship with emotional baggage feeling more like a trunk than a carry-on bag, and filled with all the emotions they have accumulated and never released because they haven't felt safe enough— a situation that drove Katherine and Matt to begin working with me soon after they were engaged to be married. Having already worked with me as a single woman, Katherine was committed to sustaining a soul-hearted partnership with herself. Now she wanted to share this experience of physical, emotional, and spiritual intimacy in partnership with Matt.

Katherine was frustrated with Matt's patterns of avoidance and denial that surfaced in their relationship as they had in Matt's relationship with his ex-wife. Katherine thus felt mired in the past relationship residue that Matt had not responsibly completed before entering into a relationship with her. To avoid conflict at all costs, Matt constantly gave in to his ex-wife's demands, took her verbal abuse, and rarely asked for more time with his five-year-old daughter. With Katherine putting positive pressure on him to complete his past relationship, however, it became more difficult for Matt to ignore his feelings as he had done all his life since his father had abandoned him when he was seven years old.

First, Matt had to physically and emotionally complete his relationship with his ex-wife so that he could establish trust, the groundwork for emotional intimacy in his new relationship with Katherine. As I guided him through this process, he began setting clear boundaries about picking up and dropping off his daughter, asking his ex-wife to call before showing up at his house. In addition, he asked for more time with his daughter and initiated court orders to support his request. Finally, when his ex-wife verbally abused him on the phone or in public, he warned her to stop and hung up the phone when necessary, letting her know she needed to treat him with respect.

Matt's inner spiritual work included tracing his patterns of avoidance and denial to his childhood and releasing his unresolved grievance against his father for having abandoned him. He also recognized that no one shared feelings in his family and that he had suppressed his feelings of loss so he could temporarily become the man of the house, taking over his father's role that had been vacated. Working through these issues allowed Matt to forgive his father and heal past wounds. Consequently, Matt began releasing his patterns of avoidance and denial in his relationship with Katherine. When an issue surfaced with her, Matt would address it immediately or set a time to in the future. Once they opened a dialogue, he practiced actively listening and accepting Katherine's feelings, even when he felt like bolting. As a couple, they worked on being open and receptive to supportive feedback on patterns and issues no matter how uncomfortable they felt.

While Katherine communicated like a motorboat at a fast, direct pace toward establishing intimacy, Matt behaved more like a sailboat, taking his time meandering through the choppy waters at a much slower, more cautious pace. But despite the fact that their communication styles differed, they could see that they complemented and could assist each other in developing a deeper level of emotional and spiritual intimacy. Yet although Matt's pace was slower, Katherine supported him by acknowledging his progress in releasing his past and moving toward a new future with her. She also learned how to pause and check in with him before expressing her feelings so he could prepare emotionally for having an intimate conversation. In addition, Katherine worked on giving Matt a chance to respond before offering supportive feedback about his behavioral patterns.

As Katherine and Matt discovered, to foster deeper levels of intimacy we start by openly communicating with our partner, revealing things that are most sensitive to us. This freedom of expression does not constitute license to hurt or demean our partner, or to use our partner as a toxic dumping ground. We have to be courteous to our partner, showing that we respect them regardless of their opinion or point of view.

Interestingly, the Native American way of partnership is often depicted not as two lovers stepping out of their individual canoes into a third, but as two warriors ensuring that the canoes are connected by rainbows. Neither partner believes the other is perfect; rather there is mutual unconditional loving acceptance of each other's being.

When we can fully express ourselves emotionally and spiritually, we experience a surge of life-force energy that inspires physical intimacy. We can then have passionate sexual experiences because this energy heightens the senses and makes us less inhibited, more playful, and freer to explore our sensuality. Similarly, sexually connecting with a beloved partner opens us to deeper levels of emotional and spiritual intimacy in our relationship.

When we share physical intimacy in a soul-hearted partnership, we are aware that even though our physical body is not perfect, with its wrinkles and bumps, we feel safe and peaceful in the arms of our partner because of their love. Embarrassment and self-consciousness don't exist at this profound level of physical intimacy, only appreciation, tenderness, and care. We let go of our restraint and share our bodies freely without reservation, shame, or fear. Spontaneity and playfulness are vital in this intimate exchange of energies. To enhance our sexuality, we can undress in front of each other, share a shower or bath, give each other sensual massages, and delight in our erotic natures. In her poem "O Friend, Understand," the sixteenth-century Hindu mystical poet Mirabai describes taking such sensual pleasure: "Within the body are gardens, / Rare flowers, peacocks; the inner music; / Within the body a lake of bliss, / On it the white soul-swans take their joy."[3]

In an ego-driven union, a sexual encounter only satisfies physical, mental, and emotional needs, with the two people merely experiencing a release of energy residue or gratification through orgasm, and not union on a spiritual plane. In a soul-hearted partnership, however, the sexual act is a means of physical and emotional liberation, as well as an exchange of spiritual energy. Many mystics have maintained that during a sexual act between loving partners the two people can potentially expand their beings beyond the physical plane and become as one on a spiritual plane. In such a sacred moment, we go beyond our physical boundaries so that the sexual act actually becomes a physical expression of light energy that transcends time and space. In this type of ecstatic union, the brain ceases all chatter, egos go inactive, and there is only intuition, response, and what seems like telepathic communication.

This state of spiritual ecstasy is the focus of Kundalini spiritual practice, in which energy is directed up the spine through a system of energy centers, or chakras, from its base in the pelvic floor toward the crown of the head, culminating in altered states of consciousness and spiritual realizations. We can also channel this type of sexual energy through conscious awareness into other creative projects and aspects of our lives.

The following exercise is helpful for deepening intimacy in a relationship. Sit naked facing your partner with your bodies intertwined. Close your eyes and gently lean into each other's bodies, opening your heart and embracing your partner's heart with your energy. Slowly take your fingers and trace your partner's energy along their spine beginning at the crown of the head then sensuously move down the spine and back up again, paying attention to the vibration and expansion of your energies. Continue to surrender to each other until, no longer conscious of your physical boundaries, you have become the loving energy between you. If desired, allow this exchange of energy to develop into lovemaking; if you don't feel like making love, lie together, caress each other sensually, and communicate about your sexual preferences. Release any inhibitions so you can invent and welcome new erotic experiences. To heighten your sensuality you could listen to unfamiliar music, dance with abandon, taste unusual foods, reveal your erotic fantasies, massage each other, or try creative ways of making love. Even when sex is subdued or not perfect it transcends us beyond our mundane preoccupations. Evoking the senses through a deep caress, a soulful gaze, or the sensual timbre of a voice can transport us to an altered state of consciousness, a separate and simultaneous reality. Such sensual and sexual experiences become a rich means of sustaining a fulfilling lifestyle and discovering more about ourselves, our partner, and our relationship.

It is equally important to dedicate time alone as a couple to celebrate your partnership emotionally and spiritually. It can be easy to fall back into our patterns and comfort zones, allowing daily routines and responsibilities to become the focus of the relationship. We often think we are connecting with our partner by engaging in child or household responsibilities together. But nurturing and deepening emotional and spiritual intimacy with our partner requires dedicated time just enjoying each other and validating our partner and our relationship. Such intimate interludes, which focus on being rather than doing, provide a much-needed break from daily routines and responsibilities, restore the balance of energies needed to sustain the integrity of our relationship, and deepen all levels of intimacy. By taking time for ourselves, our partner, and our relationship, we become more present, energized, creative, and productive.

To deepen physical, emotional, and spiritual intimacy it is helpful to set aside a few minutes each day and occasionally more time, such as a weekend, to renew the energies of your partnership in a sacred sanctuary, while walking in the woods, perhaps, or sitting in a garden, sharing a special dinner at a favorite restaurant, or luxuriating in a Jacuzzi. Take the phone off the hook, board your pets, and make child care arrangements so that nothing will interrupt you from your intimate time together. Use soothing music, light candles, build a fire in the fireplace, or bring in other elements that create a romantic atmosphere. It does not matter where, when, or how these intimate retreats occur as long as our intention is to care for ourselves and our partnership without distraction.

Periodically taking such purposeful breaks keeps us more spiritually attuned to each other. As such, we become better able to respond to unresolved issues, offer supportive feedback, and foster deeper levels of physical, emotional, and spiritual intimacy.

### Cultivating Open and Clear Communication

Cultivating open and clear communication with healthy insights and supportive feedback promotes a deepening experience of trust and intimacy, catapulting both partners toward full expression of their soul potential. Amidst the stress and complications of life, even the closest soul-hearted partners at times feel misunderstood or disconnected—all the more reason to communicate openly and clearly by speaking from the heart.

Cultivating open and clear communication depends on a number of factors. First, partners must feel secure enough to be vulnerable and express their inner truths without fear of judgment or criticism. Communicating feelings and being vulnerable is not something most people find easy to do, because it requires them to face painful experiences from the past. And yet not communicating feelings and needs is likely to lead to partnership collisions. For example, one person may want closeness and try to snuggle, while the other prefers space and abruptly pulls away without communicating their need for time alone.

Second, open and clear communication depends on partners listening responsively and supportively. People tend to be more open if their partner listens well, responds meaningfully, and supports their needs. When working with couples, I often find that if one person has difficulty listening the other has trouble stating, or even knowing, what they want, so instead they complain about what the other person is failing to give them, and then they become demanding.

Third, open and clear communication necessitates being aware of our feelings and needs and having sufficient self-esteem to articulate them or ask for whatever will maintain our true being. To gain conscious awareness of our feelings and needs periodically, we can ask ourselves: "What am I feeling or needing right now, either independently or with my partner?" Once we have answers, it is best to communicate them unambiguously to our partner.

The following scenarios illustrate various nuances of open and clear communication, which can enhance the intimacy of any relationship. In the first scenario, one partner reports to the other, "I am going for a walk alone." The individual is subtly asking his partner to support his need for time alone, though he would obtain better results by stating a loving request rather than a declaration. In the second scenario, the partner asks, "I am considering taking a walk. Would you like to join me?" In this instance there are no expectations, leaving the listener free to choose without feeling excluded or pressured. In the third scenario, one partner makes a statement that implies a need for companionship, stating, "I would really like you to take a walk with me." The listener, in response, is likely to yield to the request because of the importance it seems to have for their partner.

Fourth, open and clear communication depends on a willingness to accept the other person's viewpoint, no matter how much it differs from our own. Refusal to accept a partner's personal viewpoint typically breeds resistance and arguments. You can communicate your acceptance by saying, for example, "Wow, what an interesting point of view," "I never looked at it quite that way," or "Can you tell me why you see it that way?" The more genuinely responsive you are, the more you demonstrate that you value your partner's point of view. Then you can follow up with a meaningful discussion about your various views on the subject.

It is not necessary to agree about everything, but when you disagree be sure to remain calm, tolerant, and patient, remembering that your partner's perspective is just information and does not make them right or wrong. Besides, in perceiving information only from your own narrow viewpoint, you can easily become stuck and end up defending your fixed position; then the more you dig in your heels, the more defensive you become, and the more unreceptive to your partner's needs. Eventually, you and your partner may stop listening to each other, at which point any potential for open and clear communication evaporates.

Lack of acceptance often causes partners to get caught in an emotional eddy, whirling around and around with no resolution in sight. One indication of lack of acceptance in a relationship is bickering or blaming. Another indication is a breakdown of all real communication, leaving only reaction/reaction, with undercurrents of annoyance. Upon identifying such an impasse, release any investment you have in your position, let down your armor, and realize that there is no battle to be won or anything to prove—other than sustaining the value of your partnership.

Some guidelines for cultivating open and clear communication in a relationship are the following. First, create a safe environment in which to explore heart-to-heart communication. A safe environment consists of a space where you can be loving, nonjudgmental, trustful, and potentially enter into deep levels of intimacy with the other person. Its safety is maintained by your willingness to listen without interruption, offer honest feedback when asked, and trust the other person not to take anything personally, make assumptions, or draw conclusions. You can establish this sense of safety at the outset by asking permission to speak freely, without fear of rejection or judgment; by sharing your honest feelings without blaming or attacking your partner; and by using phrases such as "I feel," instead of "You make me feel," then supporting your partner doing the same. Throughout, whatever feelings come up must be acknowledged as the person's own valuable and meaningful experience.

When communicating in your safe environment, it is important to distinguish between supportive feedback, information to be conveyed about your partner or the relationship, and material to be released or vented for personal reasons. To use your energies productively, only share information that is beneficial to your partner's spiritual growth, and avoid causing your partner embarrassment. Also present information in a kind and respectful way that validates your relationship. As suggested in the book *Spiritual Relationships*, "Sincere, sweet words are nectar to thirsty souls."[4] Ultimately, when you share an observation or give advice to your partner with unconditional love, you open to divinely sourced information that has the potential to take your relationship to a deeper level of physical, emotional, and spiritual intimacy.

To communicate most effectively in your safe environment and prevent misunderstandings, first write down what you want to say, read it to yourself, and then revise it as necessary, omitting words that suggest blame, resentment, or defensiveness, before sharing it with your partner. And when preparing to release material that is toxic to your system, be considerate of your partner by asking if it is a good time to vent, so they can prepare to support you.

Second, clarify expectations about roles and needs before communicating. For example, preface verbal communication by saying you want your partner to function more as a sounding board than an advisor, or you want permission to speak freely about a situation that has been troubling you. Clear announcements of your expectations minimizes your partner's likelihood of judging, opening the way for supportive listening and empathy. If it becomes difficult for your partner to continue listening, pause and table the discussion until later. Resume when both of you are calm and ready to listen.

Third, check in with your partner after clearing any reactions so you can both process the communication. It is helpful to ask questions such as "What is my reaction helping me see about myself or my partner?" "What is the source of my reaction?" and "Why did I react to the situation in this particular way?" Such questions can jumpstart a release of patterns or grievances followed by a healthy discussion.

Fourth, to prevent hurt feelings or the festering of negative energy, resolve any disagreement before ending the conversation. This involves asking your partner whether or not they feel complete with the discussion so you can move in a new direction. When necessary, give each other time to process any new information. Once you and your partner have agreed that you are complete with the issue at hand, honor this agreement and do not use it to fuel a later argument. Resolving a grievance allows you to remain open with each other so your relationship is continuously evolving and your energies are available for creation.

The following story exemplifies the cultivation of open and clear communication and the resolution of disagreement. My clients Allison and Justin came to me with a desire to deepen all levels of intimacy, which required learning open and clear communication. During one of our sessions, which created a safe environment in which they could practice, they wanted to discuss their plans to buy a house together. Justin preferred to take his time looking at houses and researching many possibilities. Allison, on the other hand, had found the house of her dreams and was ready to make an offer on it. As uncomfortable as she was with Justin's more logical, cautious approach, he was just as uneasy with what he considered her impulsivity.

This major difference in how they approached decision making caused arguments between them and inhibited open communication. Whenever they discussed their points of view, Allison observed within her physical cues of anxiety and old patterns of abandonment and control that had been triggered by Justin's reluctance to immediately buy the house. The more out of control she felt, the more she tried to control him by cajoling him into making an offer on the house she wanted.

I encouraged Justin to open his heart, recognize and release his pattern of passive resistance, and let go of any reaction. His irritability cued him to release his patterns of resistance and defensiveness. Without taking Allison's reaction personally, he calmed down so he could interact with her openly and clearly. Being spiritually centered allowed him to stay lovingly connected with Allison while simultaneously detached from the patterns that had surfaced.

Allison felt supported when Justin responded in this way. And, through using expanded conscious awareness, she was able to move toward releasing her insecurity. Their ability to let go of the outcome and entertain each other's perspective not only deepened their intimacy but also encouraged open and clear communication. Through this harmonious process, they were able to listen and discuss the elements that each of them wanted in a house. Ultimately, their discussion led to letting go of the house that Allison wanted for a better option a few months later that accommodated both of their needs.

Finally, open and clear communication emerges from the practice of harmonious negotiating, which entails choosing peaceful solutions and not letting the partners' negative patterns interrupt the flow of their combined energies. While open and clear communication requires both partners to remain detached from expectations and receptive to all possibilities so as not to constrict cocreation, harmonious negotiation fosters receptivity to new information and encourages both partners to let go of unhealthy patterns, consider alternative points of view, and entertain innovative solutions so they can generate a more inspired outcome together.

In many relationships, partners spend much of their time negotiating with each other because of the multitude of choices we are presented with daily. The simplest ones involve daily tasks, such as who is going to pay the bills or walk the dog, what is for dinner, and who is doing the dishes. More complicated choices revolve around living circumstances or family matters, such as where to live, whether to have children, or who will be the bread-winner. With so many choices to make in a relationship, negotiating becomes an art that needs to be practiced. And the successful practice of harmonious negotiation depends on several elements: acknowledging the needs and desires of your partner, remaining receptive to all possibilities and communicating heart to heart, accepting your partner's point of view without reacting to or diminishing it, and being flexible so the negotiation doesn't get bogged down in irritation or resentment.

Let's look at some examples of negotiating choices in relationships. Suppose your partner spontaneously calls you on a Saturday afternoon and asks you if you would like to go out for dinner later. This seems like a simple request requiring a simple answer, but in most relationships it calls for harmonious negotiations to avoid bickering and circular arguments. Before answering your partner's question, consider how you want to spend the evening. If you have no strong preference, think about yielding to your partner's suggestion. Supporting your partner's preference shows that you are flexible and considerate of your partner's needs as well as your own. Yielding, when done not out of a pattern of obligation is a powerful choice. If, on the other hand, you do have a preference, truthfully communicate it to your partner. This opens the door to honest dialogue so you can harmoniously negotiate a compromise that takes into consideration both partners' desires. Such negotiation can lead to more inspired possibilities than either of you could have generated alone.

Yielding to the other person's choice out of a sense of obligation is not harmonious negotiation but usually reflects patterns of insecurity and seeking approval. For instance, suppose your partner asks you, "Where would you like to eat dinner tonight?" Having a preference but fearful of upsetting your partner or instigating a conflict, you might say, "I don't care. You choose." Subsequently, your partner makes a choice, but irritated at yourself for not having spoken up, you show disappointment about your partner's selection. Afterward, you and your partner bicker back and forth, creating so much tension that neither of you wants to go to dinner anymore.

When both partners instead maintain flexibility, they encourage responding rather than reacting, which keeps positive energy flowing. Then they can use shared conscious awareness to access information about their existing patterns and begin to make adjustments. Such developments are crucial for negotiating choices in which both partners realize their dreams.

**When partners establish a foundation of reciprocal absolute trust, they can add new spiritual dimensions to their relationship. Trusting ourselves and our partner, we can let down our guard and reveal our innermost being to our partner, joining together physically, emotionally, and spiritually to embrace new possibilities for the future.**

1. *Assess the degree of reciprocal trust in your relationship.* Do you and your partner relate more to each other from your insecurities than from your true beings? Are you afraid to be open, honest, and vulnerable with each other? Do you constantly seek reassurance from each other or express jealousy? If so, try to understand the roots of such behavior.

2. *Establish an environment of reciprocal absolute trust by treating your partner with respect and consideration.* Constantly recognize and release negative patterns that undermine trust, such as mean-spirited comments and negative venting. Ask yourself these questions: "Am I critical or judgmental of my partner?" "Do I blame my partner as a way of deflecting my own feelings of inadequacy?" "Do I rehash past situations or issues?"

3. *Assess whether you are deepening your levels of intimacy with your partner.* Are you able to take off your ego-induced armor and surrender your identity structure, allowing yourself to be vulnerable in each other's presence? Are you able to communicate clearly and truthfully? Are you able to be uninhibited in physical intimacy? If not, explore the basis of your guardedness or inhibition.

4. *Practice allowing yourself to be vulnerable with your partner to promote deeper levels of intimacy.* Write about your vulnerabilities in a journal, then read the passages to your partner and discuss them. Even though you may feel uncomfortable revealing your fears, desires, strengths, and weaknesses, show trust in yourself and your partner by freely expressing your concerns. Listen to your partner's response without judgment. Repeat the exercise reversing roles.

5. *Eliminate patterns that undermine intimacy.* During times of intimacy, notice any patterns undermining your ability to be vulnerable and share reciprocal absolute trust with your partner.

6. *Practice deepening physical intimacy in your relationship.* Sit naked facing your partner with your bodies intertwined. Close your eyes and gently lean into each other's bodies, embracing your partner's heart with your energy.

7. *Sustain all levels of intimacy in your relationship by dedicating sacred time for private retreats.* Take a break from daily responsibilities by going on a private retreat together. Check into a lovely hotel or simply stay home for a day or week-

end with your favorite indulgences available, such as wine, food, and bubble bath or massage oil. Let the retreat activities unfold spontaneously.

8. *Practice being fully present with your partner.* To nurture intimacy, be spontaneous and play with your partner even when doing mundane tasks together. Be mindful that teamwork gets jobs done faster than micromanagement does, and is simultaneously a means of bonding.

9. *Explore and heighten your sensuality and sexuality.* Taste unusual foods, massage each other, and make love in a variety of places. Transform your bedroom into an intimate sanctuary by decorating it with colors and textures that delight your senses, choosing a mattress and luxurious bedding that invite private interludes, and removing the TV or other distractions. Ask yourself if you are satisfied with your sexual experiences. If not, communicate your needs and desires to your partner.

10. *Practice communicating with your partner in ways that show an understanding of their needs and points of view.* Use such phrases as "I am considering going _____. Would you like to join me?" or "I am thinking of doing _____. What do you think of it?"

11. *Practice giving and receiving supportive feedback with your partner.* Start by focusing on minor issues and progress to major ones. Use initial statements such as "Are you open right now to my feedback?" or "May I suggest?" or "Do I have permission to speak freely?"

12. *Specify ground rules for harmonious negotiation.* To optimize flexibility and support and minimize resentfulness and controlling behavior, agree to ask your partner to speak freely without worrying that you might take any problems as personal criticism. In turn, honor your partner's differing points of view so that neither of you starts to feel irritated or resentful.

# Chapter Ten

## Soul-Hearted Partnership
## As the Shared Expression of Being

"You have bewitched me, body and soul, and I love, I love, I love you.
I never wish to be parted from you from this day on."
—JANE AUSTEN

*S*oul-hearted partnership empowers us to embrace the unknown by becoming cocreators of our reality. To enter into the union of soul-hearted partnership, both partners have to come to this joining of their hearts having already validated their own beings. Soul-hearted partnership necessitates recognizing and releasing patterns that threaten to disrupt the positive flow of our energy, allowing us to become increasingly responsive to ourselves, our partner, and our relationship. It permits us to expand beyond any conditions and expectations to fully express our true being and optimally use this powerful flow of energy to manifest our dreams.

### Three Relationships As One Energy Source

The dynamic of soul-hearted partnership is more than a relationship built on the outdated notion of two people each giving 50 percent. It consists of two power sources that together, operating at 100 percent of their capacity, make the relationship more than the sum of its partners.

Most relationships occur because individuals feel incomplete and thus choose someone to complete them, a pursuit rooted in the belief that another person has what we lack or need. The idea of finding a partner to complete us is reinforced in our society through the message that we are nobody unless we have somebody. When partners give only 50 percent of their energies to a relationship, however, there is no chance for it to ever be whole so it eventually is depleted. The only way it can be truly complete is if both partners give 100 percent by first experiencing soul-hearted partnership with themselves and then join to cocreate a soul-hearted partnership, based on an energetic integration of body, mind, and spirit that is more than the sum of its partners. Then each partner functions as a complete power source and takes full responsibility for contributing 100 percent of this creative energy to the relationship. As an energetic team, the two individuals produce an energetic integration that results in additional power.

We can better understand the dynamic of soul-hearted partnership by thinking of it in terms of three points of a triangle. Imagine yourself as one point and your partner as another point, then draw a line connecting the two points. Now envision these two points—each representing an individual experience of soul-hearted partnership—connected to the third point of the triangle, representing the shared experience of soul-hearted partnership. Like compound interest, which is based on the original principal plus any interest that has accrued as the principal grows, soul-hearted partnership builds not only on 100 percent of each partner's energy but also on their combined energies. Sustaining such an energetic dynamic is a key to enhancing life, both as an individual and as part of a couple.

The following vignette portrays two individuals, each sustaining a soul-hearted relationship with themselves as the basis for cocreating a soul-hearted partnership. Clients John and Christy began a relationship following the unexpected death of John's first wife. For John, age thirty-six, entering into such a partnership required him to release and complete his past relationship. Rather than grieving after his wife's death, however, he had suppressed his painful feelings and found a quick fix by embarking on a lifelong fantasy of exploring the Amazon River. While sitting alone for hours in a canoe, he was forced to confront his feelings of loss and sadness. But after his return, his grieving was interrupted by caring for his dying mother.

Within the first six months of beginning a relationship with Christy, John purchased a house and began an extensive renovation project, which became a means for transcending his painful past. While stripping away layers of paint and uncovering the structure's original handcrafted woodwork, he was simultaneously peeling away his own layers of loss and revealing his true being.

During this period of transformation, John took the time and space he needed to release his grief and heal his past. Feeling a profound sense of loss, he sometimes became depressed and wanted to be alone. In these times of his purposeful solitude, Christy discovered how to support him without making him feel guilty, and trusted that if the relationship was right for her she would want to see John continue to transform. Through his self-healing, John used his grief as a springboard for spiritual growth.

While John was renovating his house, Christy, who had recently been divorced, completed projects she wanted to finish in her home. As she spent time alone and with him, she learned to recognize and release subtle layers of her patterns of control and self-sacrifice. In a state of healthy detachment, she watched to make sure he was not expecting her to rescue him and that he was building a secure relationship with himself.

As Christy continued observing John taking responsibility for his grief, she witnessed him fulfilling his own needs, directing his energies more positively, and becoming more loving. Christy saw that they were growing both separately and together, completing their own personal business while at the same time nurturing a mutually supportive partnership.

As John and Christy's story reveals, soul-hearted partnership often evolves out of what may look like endings but are actually new beginnings. The combined energies of both partners cocreate a synergetic atmosphere of expansion, and their connection at the soul level allows them to be fully expressed as human beings.

*The Twin Flames of Full Self-Expression*
The energetic integration of two fully expressed beings is like twin flames merging to form the essence of soul-hearted partnership. What transforms an otherwise good relationship into a soul-hearted partnership is the willingness of the partners to learn to fully express themselves and spiritually grow, then share their energy of self-expression and cocreate a more fulfilling future.

As the twin flames of full self-expression merge in a relationship, the partners become a collective conduit for channeling this energy source. And forming an energetic team, they became aware of their inherent ability not only to cocreate their heart's desires but also to transcend any problems that come up in life. D. H. Lawrence paints a poignant image of this soul union when he writes, in *Women in Love*, of "star equilibrium," the symmetry established by two lovers radiating as separate stars in a constellation of devotion.[1]

Like a stove burner, to sustain its flame, relies on gas running through a pipe, soul-hearted partnership depends on a continuous, positive flow of energy to manifest the couple's individual as well as shared intentions. This energy is continuously generated when partners fully trust their connection to source and express themselves, both individually and in unison. Once generated and channeled, it creates a force for cocreation that the individuals are unable to access individually outside of the relationship.

The account of my clients Lee and Brian is a good example of how we can tap and direct this combined energy to cocreate individual and shared intentions. Because Lee's mother had muscular dystrophy, she was physically and financially dependent on Lee's father for most of their married life. And Lee, instead of receiving nurturing and guidance from her mother, helped her father take care of her. As a result of these early experiences, Lee began to believe that unconditional love and life force energy were in short supply.

Determined not to be powerless like her mother, and unconsciously equating financial reserves with life force energy, Lee sought financial independence early on. By the time I met her, in her late thirties, all her career choices had been driven by an intense need for financial success. With my guidance, however, Lee became painfully aware that her job as an accountant for a Fortune 500 company was no longer fulfilling for her.

After listening to her heart to learn what she truly wanted, Lee was drawn to the healing arts. And while terrified to leave her job in the interest of pursuing her dream of becoming a massage therapist, she knew that spiritually she had already let go of the job and begun cocreating her future by enrolling in a graduate program in massotherapy. As she followed her heart and made the discerning choices that aligned with her intention, she had to trust her connection with herself and her source, let go of her patterns of control and self-sacrifice, and allow her partner, Brian, to support her financially for the first time in her life. Significantly, she needed to accept that the power source she expressed through her heart was an important contribution to the relationship and more powerful than her corporate paychecks.

Brian, on the other hand, had grown up in a lower income household with a mentally disabled mother. Early in life, he had become accustomed to taking care of household tasks and his mother. Even with the money he made working odd jobs, there never seemed to be enough left to take care of his needs. Consequently, Brian developed a pattern of scarcity, which included a scarcity of energy. This pattern interfered with his taking steps to truly express his dreams, despite the fact that he had an advanced business degree and was financially secure.

Lee's shift from full-time work to graduate school gave Brian an opportunity to break with his pattern of insecurity by providing her with unconditional emotional and financial support. Initially, it was an uncomfortable stretch for him to care for his partner financially, but as he witnessed Lee grow, trusting herself to make choices that aligned with her true being, he felt more connected to her spiritual nature and more passionately in love with her than ever before.

With my guidance, Lee and Brian began to let go of their belief that money was security and to simultaneously release their patterns of scarcity. It was essential that they achieve a healthy relationship with money in order to attract financial abundance into their lives. As an energetic team, they had to trust that money possessed less power than the expression of their true selves within the context of their evolving partnership.

A year later, when Brian was ready to take a major step toward his desire to own a management consulting business, he followed Lee's lead and left his executive position in corporate America. Lee supported his desire and assisted him with transitional changes, such as creating a business plan, choosing office space, and recruiting clients. Merging her creative talents with his gave Lee the opportunity to support Brian's dream of owning his own business and their shared dream of living more impeccably. Like an alchemist who transforms base metals into gold, through their merged energies Lee and Brian cocreated more together than they could ever have alone, and they also learned how to support their individuality.

In contrast, while working with couples I frequently see only one person trying to ignite and sustain such positive energy flow for themselves, their partner, and the relationship. This often occurs when one partner is trying to compensate for or control the other partner, who is perceived as unable to generate their own positive energy flow. Many people want a relationship to succeed so much that they play the role of enabler or rescuer of the other person. They cajole, nag, or try to convince this person to contribute at least their fair share to the relationship and even compensate for the other person's lack of energetic input.

When only one person stokes the fire of relationship, however, it may ignite but will soon die out, leaving both partners depleted and depressed. It is not possible to make a relationship whole by compensating for the other person or by attempting to become the "other half." For a relationship to be fulfilling, each participant must contribute 100 percent of their energy to it and to every other aspect of their lives, such as taking care of the children or a pet, learning a new language, cooking dinner, talking to a friend, and even taking a shower.

Although soul-hearted partnership thrives on this unification of energies, it does not erode the individuality of each partner but rather amplifies it by fostering a healthy balance of contact and personal space. Kahlil Gibran, in his book *The Prophet,* depicts this sort of individuation when he states, "But let there be spaces in your togetherness, and let the winds of the heavens dance between you."[2] It is an individuation that encourages partners to appreciate each other's interests and aspirations without becoming carbon copies of each other.

Among the factors that impede full self-expression in a soul-hearted partnership are several misconceptions about individuality in general. One is the mistaken belief that individualized partners with separate experiences have license to do whatever they wish, regardless of the cost to the other partner. In reality, they are instead expected to honor their partner's unique-ness while also showing consideration for the person's needs and desires. Full self-expression must occur concurrently with consideration of one's partner.

Another factor impeding self-expression is the myth of compatibility—the notion that individuals who are in relationship must share everything, have all of the same interests, and make all of the same choices. For exam-ple, a young woman dating a man might pretend to enjoy sailing, but then later, as his wife, reports that she never really liked sailing and had always been seasick. Or one partner might forgo a favorite hobby and instead take up golf because their mate enjoys it. In contrast, some individuals feel threat-ened by their partner's dedication to a hobby, friends, or even personal growth; and instead of balancing their own personal needs and interests with their dedication to the relationship, they become resentful of the time their partner spends with others.

Although soul-hearted partners do need to share some common inter-ests through which they can express their energies together, they also have to remain true to their individual interests. Thus, compatibility does not mean blind compliance with a partner's involvements but rather energetic align-ment with the partner and a shared outlook on life that generates core val-ues mutually beneficial to each person's mission in life and soul progression. Such core values include freedom of expression, absolute trust, uncondi-tional love, passion, intimacy, integrity, and spiritual growth. Together, part-ners develop a love for these ideals, in conjunction with honoring their own true being.

A related misconception is the unhealthy and unrealistic expectation that partners should fulfill all of each other's needs and desires. We set our-selves up for disappointment by thinking that one person can fulfill our every need and desire. In addition to a partner, it is essential to have others in our lives who fulfill important functions, such as a spiritual friend, a shopping buddy, a workout partner, an art gallery or movie friend or colleagues with whom we work. Such friends bring out our individuality, which in turn enhances our creative contribution to our partnership, deepens our passion and intimacy, and assists in our spiritual development.

Maintaining a steady balance between spending time alone or with friends and devoting time to shared activities with our partner is crucial to establishing full self-expression in a fulfilling partnership. It is healthy for each individual to spend time alone or with friends, if only to commune with themselves. Brief activities such as a walk in the park or quietly reading a good book may satisfy the need to be alone. Longer periods alone or with friends are just as important; for instance, one partner may pursue a special interest that takes them on an ecological trip, a service project overseas, or a spiritual retreat. In soul-hearted partnership, the other partner supports these immersions so as not to limit their mate's full self-expression.

Many couples pursue their own interests and follow their own dreams in tandem with each other. For instance, one partner will stay home and care for the children to support their partner's wish to write a book, while at a later time, the author will care for the children so their partner can start a business. In this way, each person supports the choices of the other, reinforcing their partner's evolving individuality and self-expression.

Through such mutual exchanges of support, partners not only enhance each other's true beings but also help each other vanquish fears and achieve personal goals. Whereas outside the relationship some individuals might previously have procrastinated, felt apathetic, or been unfocused, they are now able to accomplish their objectives with ease. One supportive glance, word, or touch from your partner can be all it takes to inspire you to follow your heart.

With the twin flames of full self-expression merged as one energy source, partners can cocreate opportunities for producing fulfillment, both individually and as a couple, with support and gratitude yet without expectations. For example, you do not expect that your partner has made dinner or kept the house clean but are appreciative when you see he has done this. Or sensing that you need a personal break, your partner arranges for you to have special time away from responsibilities. Or your partner expresses a desire to travel with her father to Alaska, and although this is a region you would like to visit, you support her choice to go without you.

The energetic exchanges sustaining soul-hearted partnerships generate a win-win-win situation for both individuals, the couple, and others in the world who come into contact with this powerful energy source. Bill and Melinda Gates demonstrate how partners can positively direct their combined energies into the world. Although powerful as individuals, they have become even more empowered after merging their energies to cocreate the Gates Foundation, a charitable organization that assists millions of people in the world. Similarly, First Lady Michelle and President Barack Obama together set in motion their intention of having Barack become president of the United States, ushering in an era of racial equality never before known in this country. Images of the Obamas laughing with each other, holding hands, and tapping fists give us a glimpse of what this power source looks like in relationship. By joining energies they succeeded in fulfilling their dream and our nation's dream of restoring confidence in government, as can be seen in the million-plus faces televised at the inauguration in January 2009.

When the twin flames of two fully expressed beings merge, their unification of energies takes them beyond any objective they could have achieved on their own. Such outcomes can be seen over and over again throughout history, and are attributable to a commitment to core values, expanded perspectives, trust in one's connection with a divine source, and responsible choices that support both individual and global transformation.

### The Transformative Power of Combined Energies

Using the transformative power of combined energies is similar to walking on stepping stones across a stream. First, we have to release old habits, including grievances and preconceived ideas about how our intentions evolve, while simultaneously opening and joining hearts with our partner. Then we must channel the combined energies positively, making a series of discerning choices that align with our shared intentions. When partners align their energies and trust their connection to a divine source, an energetic vibration begins emanating from their shared heart centers, which then becomes a catalyst for cocreation. At this point both partners are able to view life as a blank canvas of possibilities on which they may paint their individual and shared intentions to produce an exquisite portrait of a more fulfilling future.

Not surprisingly, aligning intentions and making discerning choices to support them can be difficult if both partners have patterns of fear and scarcity. In such instances, partners my limit their imaginations and behave as if few choices were available. For example, they may insist on seeing all of Europe in ten days as opposed to realizing they could take several trips to

Europe over a longer period of time. Or partners might buy the first sofa they see, settling for an inferior product for fear that they may not find what they would really like. Or they may forgo an optimal move to a new home or job because they are afraid of changing the status quo of their relationship.

Even if only one partner has patterns of fear and scarcity, it can obstruct the alignment of intentions and discerned choice-making in a relationship. In such a scenario, the unaffected partner might want to change the energy of the living room by moving furniture, painting the walls a new color, or adding beautiful draperies, while the other partner resists, saying, "I like the living room the way it is" or "We can't afford to do this." To move beyond this impasse, the resistant partner could acknowledge the other's point of view with loving acceptance and reply, "Oh, what an interesting idea," or "Could you describe the options you see?" Aligning with your partner to make choices from a non–fear-based perspective sparks energetic teamwork, causing the job to get done faster, with less effort and more enjoyment.

When making choices in soul-hearted partnership it helps to honor each individual's spiritual progression as well as the progression of the relationship. Ultimately, striking a harmonious balance may mean either moving in sync toward the same choice, making separate choices, negotiating a new choice together, or yielding to one partner's choice. Each option might require the individuals to write down their vision of how they see a shared intention manifesting, highlight the elements most meaningful to them, then tell their vision to each other, listening without interruption and each accepting their partner's point of view. Ideally, they will incorporate into their mutual vision the essential elements identified by each partner, peacefully negotiating any necessary choices. Using this tool repeatedly will underscore for each partner the value of their individual points of view and concerns, while clearing a path to a shared intention.

The following story demonstrates the transformative power of combining energies, aligning intentions, and making discerning choices in soul-hearted partnership. Doug and I had an intention to manifest an exquisite engagement experience. As we began a two-week trip through Italy, we declared our intention and opened to the possibility of becoming engaged. We expanded our conscious awareness so we could observe the myriad of choices before us and choose well from among them.

Through our expanded conscious awareness, Doug and I each took full responsibility for our thoughts, feelings, and choices as we traveled together. We paid close attention to any new information as it emerged, and supported each other in recognizing and releasing fear-based patterns that might interrupt the positive flow of our combined energies. Directing our energies as positively as possible, we made carefully discerning choices so our shared intention would become reality.

Prior to leaving on our trip, Doug had chosen an engagement ring for me, which he'd carried with him. Releasing any attachment to how, when, and where he would propose, he remained receptive to all possible options. He knew that to bring about his true intention he would have to be as flexible as possible and trust that the timing and setting would be revealed. Likewise, I had to let go of any expectation that he would propose to me as we enjoyed Rome, Florence, and Venice together. With no attachment to a schedule or plan of how our shared intention might manifest, we followed the guidance of spirit through our hearts, moving spontaneously from moment to moment, all the while cocreating the foundation for a loving soul-hearted partnership.

Our last day in Florence unfolded with ease—a major guidepost that made us realize we were channeling our shared energies. Trusting this, we let go of our plans and opted to spend an extra night in Florence. We were amazed to see our shared intention supported by external events. We were able to easily exchange our train tickets for new ones without any additional fees. And the hotel we had reserved in Venice offered to cancel our prior reservation with no penalty.

As we dressed for dinner that evening in Florence, I felt a powerful connection between myself and Doug, sensing that we had stepped into the heart of cocreation. I experienced a heightened awareness and sensitivity to everything around me, reminiscent of a newborn. It felt like a continuous flow of energy was moving in and around our bodies, causing us to float in a crystal cocoon of light energy. When I touched Doug's face, I felt an electric current through my entire body that I knew was the energy of pure love. Stunned by this experience, I intuited that I was making a series of choices likely to shift my life completely. In that split second, I felt compelled to look at the clock beside the bed. The time was 7:12 p.m.

Having no conscious recollection of how I found my way to the lobby of the hotel that evening, I thought it could just as well have been by magic carpet. The first image I clearly remember is seeing Doug holding the car door open for me as I was mesmerized by the sheer beauty of his being. While walking toward him, I felt I was passing through an energetic threshold, and glancing at my watch I saw it had stopped at 7:12 p.m.

At dinner, the lights in the room felt soft, as if they had been dimmed. Through the filmy veil of my awareness, I noticed the waiter delicately balancing a sterling silver covered platter on his arm. When he presented it to me, I felt everything around me temporarily disappear.

Lifting the silvery lid, the waiter exposed a beautifully decorated cake. Nestled in the frosting was a ring, and under it the words "Will you marry me?" I gazed lovingly at Doug and spoke from my heart: "Yes." I knew then that our shared intention had manifested, as well as the bedrock of a soul-hearted partnership.

Soul-hearted partnership requires you and your partner to maintain the integrity of the partnership and channel combined energies to cocreate a fulfilling relationship expressing both individual and shared intentions. Once a soul-hearted partnership has been established and sustained, together the partners can project their combined energies into their surroundings to bring about positive transformation for each other and the world.

### Celebrating Soul-Hearted Partnership

Celebrating soul-hearted partnership takes place on three tiers at once. Both partners maintain their fullest sense of self as their priority. Opening to more expanded levels of conscious awareness, they observe themselves and their partner. Simultaneously they also witness their relationship from a more expanded point of view. Constantly listening to the voice of spirit through their hearts and remaining flexible, they sustain the integrity of all three perspectives. Just as in a set of Russian wedding rings each individual ring fits smoothly with the others to create the whole, the three energies of soul-hearted partnership intertwine seamlessly to nurture the whole.

The following story illustrates how my clients Sam and Jesse integrated the three energies of soul-hearted partnership as they celebrated their wedding day, and also how letting go of specific outcomes can lead to spontaneity, play, and the joy of serendipitous events. Jesse and Sam shared the intention to cocreate a private, spiritual ceremony reflecting their dedication to soul-hearted partnership. A month before, Jesse had asked me if I knew anyone who could marry them. Aware of the sacred experience they wanted to share with each other, I suggested that my colleague Bryan and I would be honored to guide this experience.

The ceremony was to take place in Santa Fe, New Mexico, on August 14. Our plan was to create an experience that could be modified extemporaneously. Bryan had asked a friend, David, for the use of his house and garden for the ceremony and another friend, Terry, if he would take photographs. With absolute trust that one moment would unfold perfectly into the next, Sam and Jesse arrived in Santa Fe the evening before their wedding day.

The next morning, Bryan and I picked them up at their hotel and drove them to an impromptu breakfast at a favorite restaurant known for its bakery. We were about to be seated in a noisy section upstairs when we decided to wait for a different table, having been told it would be a half hour. But within five minutes an intimate table became available with a view of the bakery. The four of us, as if going through the back of the wardrobe in *The Chronicles of Narnia*, were prepared to trust the people we would meet, the events that would take place, and how our intentions would manifest. Consequently, what started as simply a better choice evolved into a series of choices that strung together like an exquisite strand of pearls, creating a celebration of life.

After breakfast, as we drove Jesse and Sam to obtain their marriage license, Jesse asked us to check on flowers for the ceremony. While waiting for them to obtain their license, Bryan phoned a few of his favorite florists, finding one that was available to design a floral bouquet and boutonnière. License in hand, we drove to the florist, and even though the wedding designer was busy with another order he took the time to make up exactly what the couple had chosen.

Continuing the celebration, we drove from the center of Santa Fe to Ten Thousand Waves, a spiritually inspired Japanese spa. Jesse and Sam had made appointments there for a couple of days later, so they welcomed the advance orientation. While meditating by the koi pond, Bryan and I guided Jesse and Sam to open their hearts to each other and begin making discerning choices about the prospect of sharing their lives.

After leaving the spa for their hotel, the car sputtered and, as we pulled along the side of the road, stopped dead. As we sat in the inert car laughing and making jokes, no one got upset; we just continued in the flow of the energy that had set the tone for this special day. Realizing that we had broken down only five minutes from Sam and Jesse's hotel, Bryan brought out a phone book he kept in the car, and we called for help: the insurance company to arrange for a tow truck, a cab to take us to the nearby hotel, and a friend to assist us. This co-incident gave us the opportunity to let go of attachment to specific outcomes and sustain the flow of energy even in challenging circumstances, a sort of dress rehearsal for those Sam and Jesse were likely to face in their future.

Sam, Jesse, and I took a cab to the hotel and picked up their rental car, their wedding clothes, and the flowers, while Bryan went with the tow truck and then home. In sync still, we arrived at Bryan's home within minutes of each other, with no time lost or any event interrupted. While Bryan and I picked up our change of clothes for the ceremony, Jesse and Sam relaxed, filling their senses with Bryan's eclectic collection of art, playing with crystal Tibetan singing bowls, and enjoying the thunderstorm that had begun. For Jesse and Sam, it was a firsthand experience in listening to their hearts with absolute trust, letting go of expectations about how the day should be, and expanding beyond the conventional bubble of a wedding ceremony.

We proceeded in Jesse and Sam's car to the site of the formal ceremony, at which point the sun came out and a beautiful rainbow lit the way. We arrived at David's home in the hills and created a quiet intimate time before the ceremony for Jesse and Sam to reverently acknowledge each other. We sat on the floor with Sam and Jesse facing each other and asked them to gaze into each other's eyes, experiencing their soul, then guided them through tantric exercises. While Bryan and I played Tibetan crystal singing bowls, they opened fully to each other and experienced unconditional love as a bond between them.

As Sam and Jesse basked in the afterglow of this experience, Terry and David arrived. We meandered outside to the garden and fishpond, allowing time to ease into the ceremony.

While Sam and Jesse prepared for their wedding, David, Terry, Bryan, and I created a setting for the nuptials, placing an oriental rug on the portal floor, moving furniture, and arranging candles, angel sculptures, and flowers. Through our combined energies, we fashioned a peaceful, beautiful environment for Jesse and Sam to celebrate their sacred union.

As I waited with Sam, Bryan escorted Jesse from the house and onto the portal. We spoke to their hearts and addressed the sacred covenant they were entering into, saying:

> Reflect on that first moment when you gazed deeply into each other's eyes and were bewitched body, heart, spirit, and soul. You fell in love. It was the light in your eyes and language of your hearts that communicated your soulful connection. Heart to heart and soul to soul, you felt a spark of energy that struck a deeper chord of recognition, so pure and natural, beyond what you ever imagined.
>
> As two individuals, you are cocreating an amazing heart-and-soul-connected partnership together. You are combining forces to

bring about peace, harmony, and inspiration for yourselves and everyone around you. Your relationship will also magnify beauty in the world. As you gracefully yield to your connection, you will experience the flow of love that invites your spirits to unite and play. Combining these energies and expressing your love unconditionally, you are opening your future to be all that you want it to be.

Take your shared covenant and direct your loving flow of energy to expand into your everyday experience. See your hearts entwining in unison, opening you to endless possibilities. Envision your hearts joined, willing to share and expand the creative opportunities in your future. As you nurture and tend to each other's needs, express your love fully and often. The power of your love will sustain you—celebrate that love forever.

Your union is a beginning of commitment and the continuing validation that you are more powerful now that you are partners. Reflect on this often and on the fact that your partnership is based on this loving foundation as best friends. Trust yourselves and yield to each other and all you create together. Bless your hearts, and may your love in relationship be a lifetime of fulfillment for each of you.

As Jesse and Sam spoke their vows, professing their love of each other, two hummingbirds hovered near them. And we all celebrated the flow of positive energy that had characterized the entire experience.

**Soul-hearted partnership invites infinite opportunities for us to walk in grace every day. Rooted in the heart and soul, it insists that we live fully realized and self-expressed. And from our potent life force energies, we arouse passion, beauty, and sensuality. As such, immersed in this sacred relationship we experience not only a deepening physical, emotional, and spiritual intimacy but also our own and our partner's soul progression.**

PRACTICING THE PRINCIPLES IN CHAPTER TEN

1. *Assess the dynamic of your soul-hearted partnership.* Consider the following: Are you staying true to yourself while in the relationship? Is your partner sustaining his or her true self while in relationship with you? Are you and your

partner balancing your individual energies while contributing 100 percent of your energies to the relationship?

2. *Write down and share with your partner your vision of the partnership now, in six months, in a year, and in five years.* What intentions do you have individually? What intentions do you share? How do you see you and your partner cocreating these intentions for each of you individually and for your partnership?

3. *Honor individual interests and aspirations in your partnership.* Support each other's full self-expression by welcoming individual choices without jealousy, resentment, or insecurity. Encourage your partner to spend the necessary time alone to sustain full self-expression by going on a retreat, taking a yoga class, visiting art galleries, or traveling. Be understanding of your partner's need for individual expression to maintain the integrity of your partnership.

4. *Determine whether all three relationships are in balance in your partnership.* Ask yourself: "Are my energies being used optimally to nurture myself, my partner, and our partnership?" If you determine that your energies are being directed unequally, find ways to attain better balance.

5. *Walk in a state of gratitude with your partner.* Remember to talk about your best times together. Identify experiences that made those times particularly fulfilling for each of you, and the elements that characterized them. Then integrate these elements when cocreating new experiences.

# Conclusion

## A MEDITATION FOR SOUL-HEARTED PARTNERSHIP

*E*nvision yourself walking with your partner on a magnificent beach at sunrise. The sun is slowly peeking over the horizon, signaling a new moment in your life. Sharing the rising sun with your partner, you are aware of how you feel holding hands. You are awed by the way your partner's face lights up with joy as the sun comes over the horizon, realizing that witnessing this amazing scene alone would be stirring but sharing the experience is even more inspirational.

You quietly walk side by side, making parallel footprints in the sand. You both pause and silently gaze at the ocean, looking outward together toward your future. You gently squeeze each other's hand, acknowledging the loving energy that connects your hearts and souls.

You are whole and complete. Your partner is whole and complete. Your twin flames infuse your partnership with light energy. All three relationships are nurtured simultaneously, so your partnership has power beyond the sum of its partners.

Although you are each alone, there is no feeling of separation. You are two beings connected through a divine energy source. As the sunlight reflects off the sand, you experience the full expression of the light of your beings.

You are drawn to the horizon, where a dolphin's fin breaks through the water. Your partner makes a beeline to the top of a sand dune, inviting you to share in the experience. You wave back, acknowledging your partner's invitation, but are content to stare at the sea anticipating the next black triangle to emerge. Your partner smiles at you in silent understanding of your desire. You give each other permission to fully express your own choices in the moment—separate yet deeply connected.

# Notes

## Chapter One

1. Antoine de Saint-Exupéry, *The Little Prince* (New York: Harcourt Brace & Company, 1943), 87.

2. Caroline Myss, *Anatomy of the Spirit* (New York: Three Rivers Press, 1996), 57.

3. Bryan Christopher, personal communication.

4. James Austin, *Zen and the Brain: Toward an Understanding of Meditation and Consciousness* (Cambridge, MA: MIT Press, 1999), 652.

5. Simon Peter Fuller, *Rising Out of Chaos: The New Heaven and Earth* (Cape Town, South Africa: Kima Global Publishers, 1996), 184.

## Chapter Two

1. Erich Fromm, *The Art of Loving* (New York: Harper & Row, 1956), 114.

2. John Welwood, *Perfect Love, Imperfect Relationships* (Boston: Trumpeter, 2007), 105–106.

3. D. H. Lawrence, *The Complete Poems of D. H. Lawrence* (New York: Viking Press, 1971), 449.

4. Helen Keller, *The Story of My Life* (New York: Grosset & Dunlap, 1905), 203.

5. Isaac Stern, "La musique, c'est ce qu'il y'a entre les notes," *L'Express* (December 2000): 40.

6. Anonymous.

7. George James Firmage, ed., *E. E. Cummings Complete Poems: 1904–1962* (New York: Liveright Publishing, 1979), 663.

## Chapter Three

1. Myss, *Anatomy of the Spirit*, 135.

2. Rachel Carson, *The Sense of Wonder* (New York: Harper & Row, 1956), 88–89.

*Chapter Four*

1. *Shadowlands,* directed by Richard Attenborough (Manchester, UK: Savoy Pictures, 1993).

2. Judith Viorst, *Necessary Losses* (New York: Simon & Schuster, 1986), 15–16.


*Chapter Five*

1. Gary Zukav, *The Seat of the Soul* (New York: Simon & Schuster, 1989), 106.

2. Henry David Thoreau, *Walden* (New York: T. Y. Crowell, 1854), 340.


*Chapter Six*

1. Paramhansa Yogananda, *Spiritual Relationships* (Nevada City, CA: Crystal Clarity Publishers, 2007), 21.

2. *The Mirror Has Two Faces,* directed by Barbara Streisand (Hollywood, CA: Tri Star Pictures, 1996).

3. Lawrence, *The Complete Poems of D. H. Lawrence,* 661.

4. Coleman Barks, *The Essential Rumi* (San Francisco: Harper, 2004), 106.

5. Yogananda, *Spiritual Relationships,* 58.

6. Jalal Al-Din Rumi, Jonathan Star, and Shahram Shiva, *A Garden Beyond* (New York: Bantam, 1992), 59.

7. William Roetzheim, *The Giant Book of Poetry* (Jamul, CA: Level 4 Press, 2006), 502.


*Chapter Seven*

1. Shakti Gawain, *Creative Visualization: Use the Power of Your Imagination to Create What You Want in Your Life* (Novato, CA : New World Library, 2002), 157.

2. Helen Schucman and William Thetford, *A Course in Miracles* (Mill Valley, CA: Foundation for Inner Peace, 1975), 95.

3. Jane Hirshfield, *Of Gravity and Angels* (Hanover, NH: Wesleyan University Press, 1988), 7.

4. Soren Kirkegaard, *Works of Love* (Princeton, NJ: Princeton University Press, 1995), 167.

*Chapter Eight*

1. Rainer Maria Rilke, *Letters to a Young Poet* (Novato, CA: New World Library, 2000), xii.

2. Anne Morrow Lindbergh, *Gifts from the Sea* (New York: Pantheon Books, 1975), 108.

3. Rilke, *Letters to a Young Poet*, 63.

4. Jalal Al-Din Rumi, John Moyne, and Coleman Barks, *Open Secret: Versions of Rumi* (Watsonville, CA: Threshold Books, 1984), 52.

5. Holbrook Jackson, *Southward Ho!* (Manchester, NH: Ayer, 1977), 109.

6. George Gordon Byron and William Bell Scott, "Childe Harold's Pilgrimage," *The Complete Poetical Works of Lord Byron* (Brampton, Cumberland, UK: George Routledge, 1886), 314.

7. Firmage, ed., *E. E. Cummings Complete Poems: 1904–1962*, 766.

8. Spencer Joshua Alwyne Compton Northampton, Alfred T. Jennyson, and Charles Tennyson Turner, *The Tribute: A Collection of Miscellaneous Unpublished Poems by Various Authors* (London, UK: J. Murray and H. Lindsell, 1837), 106.

*Chapter Nine*

1. Kaleel Jamison, *The Nibble Theory and the Kernel of Power: A Book About Leadership, Self-Empowerment, and Personal Growth* (Mahwah, NJ: Paulist Press, 2004), 63.

2. Ralph Waldo Emerson, *Essays: First and Second Series* (New York: Houghton Mifflin, 1903), 319.

3. Mirabai, "O Friend, Understand," *Gateway to Indian Classical Literature* (Singapore: Asiapac Books, 2005), 127.

4. Yogananda, *Spiritual Relationships*, 33.

*Chapter Ten*

1. D. H. Lawrence, *Women in Love* (Norwalk, CT: Collector's Library, 2005), 432.

2. Kahlil Gibran, *The Prophet* (Hertfordshire, UK: Wordsworth Editions, 1997), 7.

# Bibliography

Barks, Coleman. *The Essential Rumi*, San Francisco: Harper, 2004.

Bradley, Marion Zimmer. *The Mists of Avalon*. New York: Ballantine, 1982.

Calaprice, Alice. *The Quotable Einstein*. Princeton, NJ: Princeton University Press, 1996.

Emerson, Ralph Waldo. *The Essential Writings of Ralph Waldo Emerson*. New York: The Modern Library, 2000.

Firmage, George James, ed. *E. E. Cummings Complete Poems: 1904-1962.* New York: Liveright Publishing Corporation, 1979.

Foundation in Light, 3 Abanico Road, Santa Fe, NM 87505-8396.

Fromm, Erich. *The Art of Loving*. New York: Harper & Row, 1956.

Gawain, Shakti. *Creative Visualization: Use the Power of Your Imagination to Create What You Want in Your Life*. Novato, CA: New World Library, 2002.

Gibran, Kahlil. *The Prophet*, Hertfordshire, UK: Wordsworth Editions, 1997.

Lawrence, D. H. *The Complete Poems of D. H. Lawrence.* New York: Viking Press, 1971.

Lindbergh, Anne Morrow. *Gifts from the Sea.* New York: Pantheon, 1975.

Miller, Alice. *The Drama of the Gifted Child*. New York: Basic Books, 1981.

Myss, Caroline. *Anatomy of the Spirit.* New York: Three Rivers Press, 1996.

Pipher, Mary. *Reviving Ophelia*. New York: Ballantine Books, 1994.

Rilke, Rainer Maria. *Letters to a Young Poet*. Novato, CA: New World Library, 2000.

Schucman, Helen, and William Thetford. *A Course in Miracles.* Mill Valley, CA: Foundation for Inner Peace, 1975.

Viorst, Judith. *Necessary Losses.* New York: Simon & Schuster, 1986.

Welwood, John. *The Journey of the Heart: Intimate Relationship and the Path of Love.* New York: Harper Collins, 1990.

Welwood, John. *Perfect Love: Imperfect Relationships.* Boston: Trumpeter, 2007.

Yogananda, Paramhansa. *Spiritual Relationships.* Nevada City, CA: Crystal Clarity Publishers, 2007.

Zukav, Gary. *The Seat of the Soul.* New York: Simon & Schuster, 1989.

# About the Author

DEBRA L REBLE, PH.D., a licensed psychologist, conducts a private practice and facilitates workshops and seminars that focus on enhancing personal transformation and well-being. She also is the founder of HeartPaths of Cleveland, Ohio, a company dedicated to providing materials that inspire full self-expression. In addition, she is a director of Foundation in Light, an international nonprofit educational organization devoted to the integration of light through the heart into human experience. In her role as director, she assists in presenting workshops, retreats, and consultations to promote spiritual growth and self-realization.

As a child, Dr. Reble knew she was called to offer spiritual guidance. While helping to raise her two brothers and nine stepsiblings, she experienced strong intuitive capacities that she eventually channeled into her graduate studies and her later career in education, psychology, and spiritual teaching. In 1983, after completing her master's degree in early childhood development and psychology at Kent State University, Dr. Reble worked as a school psychologist. At the time, fascinated by the influence of developmental, familial, and cultural issues on women and children, she designed a comprehensive therapeutic program for inspecting family of origin issues and offering social support to women with mild to severe emotional difficulties. She then resumed her graduate studies and, in 1993, received her doctorate in psychology at Kent State University.

Married and the mother of two, Dr. Reble lives in Cleveland, Ohio, and travels extensively. In recent years, she has produced *Journey of the Heart*, an audiocassette of guided imagery and inspirational music that opens the energetic pathways of the heart, and *A Mother's Lullaby*, a CD/audiocassette designed to nourish the physical, emotional, and spiritual bonds between mother and baby. This is her first book.

## Order Form

*Quantity*                                                                      *Amount*

_____   *Soul-Hearted Partnership: Creating the Ultimate Experience of*
              *Love, Passion, and Intimacy* ($16.00 paperback, $25.00 hardcover)    _____

              Sales tax of 7% for Ohio residents                               _____

              Shipping and handling ($3.00 for first paperback and
              $1.00 for each additional paperback; $4.00 for first
              hardcover and $2.00 for each additional hardcover)               _____

              **Total amount enclosed**                                        _____
              *Quantity discounts available*

---

**Method of payment:**

❏ Check or money order enclosed (made payable to HeartPaths Media in US
   funds only)
❏ MasterCard      ❏ VISA

Credit Card #: _____
Exp.: _____

---

Ship to (please print):

NAME _____

ADDRESS _____

CITY/STATE/ZIP _____

PHONE _____

HeartPaths
Media, LLC

PO Box 181236, Cleveland Heights, OH 44118
phone toll-free 866-976-5795   fax 216-321-1921
www.soulheartedpartnership.com